Valuation approaches for corporate investments

and takeovers with a focus on small and

medium-sized enterprises (SME)

- A literature analysis -

Thomas Eulenpesch

Valuation approaches for corporate investments and takeovers with a focus on small and medium-sized enterprises (SME)

- A literature analysis -

Bibliografische Information der Deutschen Nationalbibliothek:

Die Deutsche Nationalbibliothek verzeichnet diese Publikation in der Deutschen Nationalbibliografie; detaillierte bibliografische Daten sind im Internet über http://dnb.dnb.de abrufbar.

ISBN: 978-3-944844-07-7

Autor: Thomas Eulenpesch

Lektorat: Carina Casimir

CONTENT

EXPOSÉ

Business appraisals happen daily in enterprises listed on the stock exchange. However, there are many occasions where economists need to evaluate companies, such as in lending, in business investments, in the sale or transfer of companies or in tax reasons (estate duty).

In this bachelor thesis, different methods will be presented and discussed. In view of limited financial resources and dynamically changing global market, companies must finance innovations and investment rationally and under the aspect of sustainability.

In the increasing global competition and the associated need for internationalization, economists have developed different models over the last three decades. In this work, the focus is on the evaluation of SME. Here will be a special on function-oriented appraisal systems (such as the discounted cash flow method, etc.).

In the literature, for example, economist still poorly consider the knowledge management as a factor for evaluation, although the knowhow in increasing global competition (e.g. in relation to the Asian markets) is becoming more and more a strategic factor.

1 INTRODUCTION

In this Bachelor Thesis, the business appraisal in small and medium-sized enterprises will be analyzed. There will be a special focus on the characteristics of small and medium-sized enterprises as well as the influence factors of company evaluation.

At first the characteristics of small and medium size business will be analyzed. In this way, the assessment in the size range as well as the particular characteristics of these companies will be explained.

In the third section of this Bachelor Thesis, the basics of business appraisal, in particular the company's value, the events and the requirements on the company valuation were treated in more detail.

The following section describes the different methods of business appraisal with regard to the factors of small and medium-sized enterprises. In Chapter 5, the peculiarities of real options in the company evaluation will be additionally discussed.

From the collected information, the scopes for design in the calculation of the enterprise value will be derived. This should illustrate, in particular, that the evaluator has a clear influence on the calculated amount of the company's value and therefore the value is not completely objective.

The information gathered in this Bachelor Thesis will be evaluated and recommendations for the business appraisal will be derived as well which might be a starting point for a future research.

2 SMALL AND MEDIUM-SIZE ENTERPRISES

Due to their characteristics, small and medium-sized enterprises have different requirements of management compared to big companies. Welsh and Whiteim make this obvious in shortened form on closer examination of the hypothesis from - 1980: „A small business is not a little big business".[1]

On the other hand, this hypothesis, economists can only confirm, if the small and medium-sized enterprises in different parts distinguish themselves clearly from the big companies. Concerning this, however, economists cannot detect any agreement in the science, so that no generally accepted definition of small and medium-sized enterprises exists.[2]

Because of these business matters, economists deal with different characteristics of small and medium-sized enterprises. In this way, they have to elaborate differences of these companies. In the following section, the characteristics of small

---

[1] Welsh/White, A small business is not a little big business, in: Harvard Business Review, 59/80, p. 18

[2] Sygusch, F. (2008) Nachfolgefinanzierung mittelständischer Unternehmen, p. 18ff

and medium-sized enterprises, which are of fundamental significance for the evaluation will be explained.

2.1 CHARAKTERISTICS OF SMALL AND MEDIUM-SIZED ENTERPRISES

In order to work on delineation between small and medium-sized companies and big enterprises, economists have to analyze different characteristics. On the one hand, in this case it is possible, to carry out delineation on the back of quantitative characteristics and on the other hand based on qualitative characteristics.[3]

In the qualitative characteristics for the delineation, economists use clearly quantifiable sizes. However, in a qualitative method they work with different characteristic features for the delineation of the small and medium-sized enterprises from big companies.

---

[3] Spielmann, N. (2012) Internationale Corporate Governance, p. 19

2.1.1 Qualitative Characteristics

One possibility for classification is to use a qualitative definition. In this qualitative definition, the principal focus is on the liability and property structure. Usually economists consider the definition as a medium-sized enterprise as fulfilled, if there is a good rapport between the management and the company's owner. Such a relationship exists in particular in family businesses. This also means that in the application of qualitative definition a small business cannot be a member of a corporation.[4]

Thus, the application of the qualitative definition guarantees no standard view. This is primarily because of the fact that even companies, which exceed the European Union's size classes, can belong to the middle class due to the structure. Therefore, the economist usually applies only the quantitative definition.[5]

---

[4] Wallau, F. (2006) Mittelständische Unternehmen in Deutschland, p. 13 ff

[5] Wallau, F. (2006) Mittelständische Unternehmen in Deutschland, p. 15

2.1.2 Quantitative Characteristics

There are different criteria for the classification of companies. Usually, economists resort to quantitative factors. A small or medium-sized company has to comply with at least two of three threshold values according to criteria presented in the field of sales, number of employees and total assets. However, there are different views regarding this, which we see below:

Enterprise category	Headcount	and	annual turnover
small	up to 9		up to 1 million €
medium	up to 49		up to 50 million €
SME together	below 50		below 50 million €

SME-definition of the "Institut für Mittelstandsforschung", Bonn[6]

---

[6] Institut für Mittelstandsforschung (not stated) KMU-Definition des IfM Bonn

SME-definition of the Confederation of German Bank:[7]

- small enterprises: turnover up to 500.000 EUR
- medium-sized enterprises: turnover up to 50 Mio. EUR
- big enterprises: turnover up to 500 Mio. EUR

By using these different definitions, economists can regard making a clear delineation as problematic. However, a clear definition in the context of this Bachelor Thesis is of fundamental importance. Due to the pressing legal position, I decided to use the definition of the European Union in the context of this thesis.

---

[7] IHK Berlin (not stated) Mittelstand in Berlin – Definition Mittelstand

Enterprise category	Headcount: Annual Work Unit (AWU)	Annual turnover	or	Annual balance sheet total
Medium-sized	< 250	≤ €50 million (in 1996 € 40 million)	or	≤ €43 million (in 1996 € 27 million)
Small	< 50	≤ €10 million (in 1996 € 7 million)	or	≤ €10 million (in 1996 €5 million)
Micro	< 10	≤ €2 million (previously not defined)	or	≤ €2 million (previously not defined)

SME-definition of the European Union[8]

---

[8] European Commission (2006) The new SME-definition, p. 14

2.2 SPECIAL CHARACTERISTICS OF SMALL AND MEDIUM-SIZE ENTERPRISES

2.2.1 Specific features in the Corporate Management and Structure

Most of the small and medium-sized enterprises show the special quality that in majority they are the property of the respective entrepreneur. From this result, legal and economic peculiarities are therefore in free float compared to large companies, which are usually led in the form of a joint-stock company.

This means that most owners and corporate management consist of the same people in small and medium-sized enterprises. In this way, both the corporate culture as well as the strategy, the company management uses, are affected.[9]

The fact that the existence of the manager or owner depends on his own decisions, has a significant influence on the strategy, the company management uses. Accordingly, the manager will

---

[9] Grohmann, O. (2007) Integration der Informationstechnologie, p. 35

show a lower risk-taking due to his responsibility towards himself and his employees.[10]

This means, in addition, that the respective company owner has a central role in the success or failure of the company. Thus, a possible change in corporate management can have a major influence, for example, in the context of generation succession, the company or its profit. Therefore, it is necessary to consider the corporate management in some way in the business appraisal.

Furthermore, depending on the form of enterprise, the economist must also reflect the so-called imputed wage in the business appraisal. This is particularly important in companies where the respective owner does not receive a fixed remuneration.[11]

The need to decide about the entrepreneur results in particular also from the fact that due to the relatively small numbers of employees in small and medium-sized enterprises a strong personal corporate structure exists.

---

[10] Meyer, J.-A. (ed.) (2010) Strategien von kleinen und mittleren Unternehmen, p. 433

[11] Schacht, U., Fackler, M. (ed.) (2009) Praxishandbuch Unternehmensbewertung, 2. Edition, p. 174

Often there is also the problem that the entrepreneur can show only a technical training followed by master artisan. Accordingly, these entrepreneurs are indeed competent in the technical management of the company but are not sufficient for business management, administration and development.[12]

Since most of the owners and at the same time managers undertake a variety of tasks within the company, there is a central concentration on the company's expertise. The economist must consider this in the business appraisal, since a change of management may finally emerge problems at the time of transfer. To these problems, economists commonly refer as transfer problems. However, they can also assume that nobody may shift the problems in transfer of the company out of the way.[13]

On the other hand, small and medium-sized enterprises show a distinct advantage due to short information ways when an adaptation to new circumstances on the market is necessary.

---

[12] Akademie des Handwerks an der Unterweser (ohne Angabe) Schnittstelle zwischen Büro und Werkstatt

[13] Handke, M. (2011) Die Hausbankbeziehung, p. 32

This adaptation is advantageous; inter alia, if an adaptation to the needs of particular customers is required.

Among other things, the possibility of specialization of the company results from this. Therefore, the economist must also consider this in the context of business appraisal, because despite the small size of the company, a dominant position is possible in a niche market for the company.[14]

Through the most clear and simple hierarchical structure for the respective company, an advantage in terms of flexibility can also arise. However, this structure can also have the disadvantage of lack of documentation and insufficient future planning.

Accordingly, important data, such as market analysis or detailed cost calculations for example, which the economist can use as a basis for company evaluation does not exist. In accounting often only, the data is available, which the law has strictly prescribed. Therefore, these are sometimes of limited use for the business appraisal.[15]

---

[14] Rauter, R. (2013) Interorganisationaler Wissenstransfer, p. 19ff

[15] Andreae, C. von (2007) Familienunternehmen und Publikumsgesellschaft, p. 73

2.2.2 Size-Related Characteristics

Due to the limited resources of the company, special effects and requirements arise in particular in the finance sector of small and medium-sized enterprises. Often small and medium-sized enterprises finance themselves from the equity for the most part, on average to 26.6%.[16]

Commensurately, in the business appraisal the economist must consider that the entrepreneur is one of the biggest lenders and has therefore an appropriate position of power. Furthermore, there is also the possibility that additional property items, which are necessary for the company, are part of the company's personal assets. Therefore, the economist must contemplate these in the business appraisal.

On the other hand, economics can classify the procurement of new capital, particularly equity, in small and medium-sized enterprises as problematic. This is primarily because for the small and medium-sized enterprises, in contrast to stock corporations, it is not possible to issue shares. Thus, the

---

[16] Schwarz, Dr. M. (2012) KfW-Mittelstandspanel 2012, p. 3

possibility would remain to receive a new associate, but the present single owners often don't desire this.[17]

In addition, economists classify the loan financing of small and medium-sized enterprises as problematic. This results from the fact that in comparison to large companies, small companies receive security only in a limited extent. Thus, for these, finance institutions grant either no credit or only with relatively high interest rates. When lending, banks often take the credit worthiness of the entrepreneur into account, although he does not have to be in direct contact with the company.[18]

Accordingly, the respective owner is more or less forced to invest all his capital into the company. Thus, he has little opportunity to finance in different investment options in order to spread and minimize the risk best possible.[19]

Therefore, it is necessary to consider also this matter in the business appraisal, especially in the application of capital market-orientated methods.

---

[17] Hölscher, R. (2010) Investition, Finanzierung und Steuern, p. 256

[18] Hölscher, R. (2010) Investition, Finanzierung und Steuern, p. 229

[19] Hölscher, R. (2010) Investition, Finanzierung und Steuern, p. 256

Furthermore, the economist must also take into account a connection between the individual factors in the appraisal of the respective company the economist. This means that a high level of flexibility and thus a high market adaptation would be possible, but the implementation may be limited due to lack of capital structure.[20]

[20] Burkhardt, C. (2008) Private Equity als Nachfolgeinstrument für Schweizer KMU, p. 19

3 BASICS OF THE BUSINESS APPRAISAL

3.1 DEFINITION: COMPANY VALUE

At the term "company value", we can look both, from the objective and subjective point of view. In the objective way of looking at things, economists state in the value theory, that the interests of individual subjects or purposes of evaluation are not the sources for determination of the each company's value.[21]

Accordingly, the company's evaluation occurs neither from the buyer's nor from the seller's point of view. Instead, the evaluation happens according to the possible success potentials and in consideration of the existing assets.[22]

Therefore, for the objective determination of the business value the economist can use the net asset value method. However, many scientists face this method critically. Accordingly, they

---

[21] Matschke, M. J., Brösel, G. (2005) Unternehmensbewertung: Funktionen – Methoden - Grundsätze, p. 14ff

[22] Peemöller, V. H. et Al (2004) Praxishandbuch Unternehmensbewertung, 3. Edition, p. 4ff

usually only use this method as a basis for the subjective evaluation.[23]

According to the value theory, the subjective company's value refers to the business utility or the decision value, also known as the marginal price.[24]

Accordingly, the interests of the buyer and seller have influence on the company's value. This means that each of the involved subjects have a different idea regarding the company's value. In the assessment economists always take the future net distributions of the respective company as a basis. They determine the subjective company's value usually by using the gross rental method; the economist calls this the future success value due to the focus on the future payments.[25]

---

[23] Peemöller, V. H. et Al (2004) Praxishandbuch Unternehmensbewertung, 3. Edition, p. 4ff

[24] Peemöller, V. H. et Al (2004) Praxishandbuch Unternehmensbewertung, 3. Edition, p. 6ff

[25] Peemöller, V. H. et Al (2004) Praxishandbuch Unternehmensbewertung, 3. Edition, p. 4ff

In addition to the objective and subjective ways of determining the company's value, there is also the possibility to use the functional value theory.[26]

In this method, it is necessary to divide the company into its various functions, consequently in a sector with a main and an auxiliary function. The main functions include doing the counseling, mediation and reasoning function. The auxiliary functions relate to the information, tax base and contract design functions.[27]

Accordingly, the functional value theory, the economist must determine the company's value for a potential buyer in other way as the existing partner's redundancy claim.[28]

However, the Institute of Certified Public Accountants prefers to determine the company's value on the basis of expected financial surplus paid to the owner.

---

[26] Peemöller, V. H. et Al (2004) Praxishandbuch Unternehmensbewertung, 3. Edition, p. 7

[27] Peemöller, V. H. et Al (2004) Praxishandbuch Unternehmensbewertung, 3. Edition, p. 8

[28] Peemöller, V. H. et Al (2004) Praxishandbuch Unternehmensbewertung, 3. Edition, p. 8

The economist determines the present value of this surplus by discounting with the help of the capitalization rate. Institute of Certified Public Accountants also refers to this value as the company's subjective value as a future profit value. Here, the economist applies either the gross rental or the discounted cash flow method.

3.2   THE CAPITAL ASSET PRICING MODELL

In 1960, Sharpe, Linter and Mossin developed the Capital Asset Pricing Model (CAPM). Markowitz's portfolio theory makes up the basis for the CAPM. The focus of the CAPM is directed on a reply to the question, how to evaluate risk assets on the capital market. Here, the economy establishes a connection between the accepted risk and the amount of yield.[29] Because the CAPM bases on the portfolio theory, the same conditions make up the basis. These are:[30]

---

[29] Kruschwitz, L., Husmann, p. (2012) Finanzierung und Investition, 7. Edition, p. 187

[30] Müller, A. (2008) Anlageberatung bei Retailbanken, p. 28

- The investors risk aversion
- The investors always act rationally
- Investors make the decision based on the expected values and the standard deviation of the portfolio return
- Securities are divisible
- There are no taxes or transaction costs
- There was a uniform risk-free interest rate
- There is a perfect market

In order to derive the CAPM, the economist must determine the capital market line first. It reflects the expected combination of risk and return of an efficient portfolio. In particular, those portfolios are efficient that are on the capital market line between the market portfolio and the risk-free interest rate.

The economist can classify all other combinations as not efficient as not efficient, because they bring a smaller yield at similar risk or at the same yield a bigger risk.[31]

---

[31] Damhmen, A. (2012) Investition, p. 137ff

In the portfolio-Selection-Theory the economist assumes that all Investors are risk adverse. This means, that these chose the portfolio with the lowest risk in an expected amount.

3.3 REASONS FOR BUSINESS APRAISALS

It may be necessary for various reasons to carry out a business appraisal. However, this is especially essential for the transfer of the business to the next generation or for a sale of the respective company.

Surveys suggest that about 70% of companies will transfer to the next generation or a new owner in the coming years. Based on this number, economists also see the significance of the business appraisal.[32]

However, there are also events which make a business appraisal necessary, but are not interconnected with a transfer of the business to a new owner. Commonly economists refer to them as non-transactional events. On the other hand, to the events that

---

[32] Wassermann, B. (2012) 3. FOM Mittelstandsforum: Steuern, Recht & Bewertung, p. 23

are associated with a change in ownership, they refer as transaction-related events. The economist can divide into dominated and non-dominated events.[33] This subdivision will be illustrated in the following graphic.

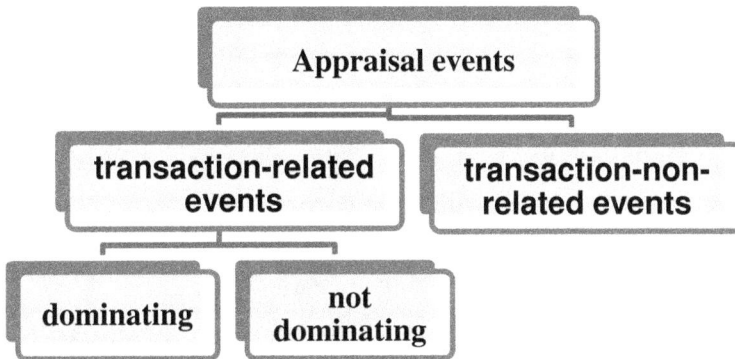

```
                    ┌─────────────────────────┐
                    │     Appraisal events    │
                    └─────────────────────────┘
            ┌───────────────┴───────────────┐
┌───────────────────────┐       ┌───────────────────────┐
│  transaction-related  │       │  transaction-non-      │
│        events         │       │  related events        │
└───────────────────────┘       └───────────────────────┘
        ┌───────┴───────┐
┌───────────────┐  ┌───────────────┐
│  dominating   │  │      not      │
│               │  │  dominating   │
└───────────────┘  └───────────────┘
```

Events of the business appraisal

In the following the possible events of business appraisal will be briefly discussed. Other facts on this are also shown in table 2.

Even if the ownership structure remains unchanged, it may be necessary to evaluate a company. This need may arise, inter alia,

---

[33] Mandl, G., Rabel, K. (1997) Unternehmensbewertung, p. 13

due to legal requirements. This includes, among other things, the business appraisal for tax purposes.[34]

Another reason for the business appraisal is the procurement of debt. This means that the relevant investor, such as a bank, requires the company's value to a credit check.

Even in a possible disturbing situation, it may be necessary for the company to prepare an insolvency plan. This refers also to the corporate restructuring, in which the corporation must carry out negotiations with the creditors.[35]

As previously mentioned, there are also transaction-related events that in turn the economist can divide into dominated as well as non-dominated events. The dominated events make it possible for one for the parties to change the ownership relations, independently, without discussion with the other party. One of the most famous dominated events is the retirement of one of the shareholders of an ordinary partnership.[36]

---

[34] Wöltje, J. (2012) Finanzkennzahlen der Unternehmensbewertung, p. 88

[35] Wöltje, J. (2012) Finanzkennzahlen der Unternehmensbewertung, p. 88

[36] Kalmar, N., Sommer, U., Weber, I. (ed.) (2013) Der effiziente M&A Prozess, p. 80

In the non-dominated events, none of the involved parties is forced to agree to the change of the ownership relations. This is particularly important in a business selling case. This means that in a possible sale the owner can cancel the negotiations at any time, for example while achieving only a fraction of the desired price.[37]

events	events, affecting transactions		transactions non related events
	Non dominated situations	dominate situations	

[37] Prätsch, U., Ludwig, E., Schikorra, U. (2012) Lehr- und Praxisbuch für Investition, Finanzierung und Finanzcontrolling, p. 371

buy, sale	Buy or sale of the company or company shares	Retirement of a partner from an ordinary partnership through - retirement of the partner (cancelling) - exclusion of an "annoying" partner - starting of bankruptcy proceedings about the partner's assets	

Compensations in money		Money compensations of majority partner in - settlement of an profit transfer or controlling agreement (§ 305 II No. 2 u. 3 AktG) - integration of majority decision (§ 320 AktG) - conversion through assets transfer (§ 174 UmwG) - modifying conversion	

		(§§ 190, 207 UmwG)	
dispossession		dispossession /socialization according to art. 14,15 GG	
Share of inheritance		Partitions of inheritances, shares of inheritances, compensations as established in family law (equalization of accrued gains)	

taxation			Estate duty, trade tax, etc.
bankruptcy			Basis for bankruptcy plans
founding	Founding of a partnership with integration of business shares		
accession	Accession of new partners in an existing partnership without departure of other partners		
fusion	Fusion according to §§ 2 ff. UmwG		

		Compensation of majority partner in stocks of the main partnership in settlement of a profit transfer or controlling agreement (§ 305 II No. 2 u. 3 AktG) - integration of majority decision (§ 320 AktG) - fusion (§§ 19, 29 UmwG)	
compensation in stocks			

3.4 REQUIREMENTS OF THE BUSINESS APPRAISAL

In the business appraisal, the fundamental problem lies in the fact that there are no binding legal norms and thus it it is optional for each reviewer, which methods to use.

At this point, Adolf Moxter tried to introduce a generally accepted standard, similar to the principle of proper accounting, known as principle of proper business appraisal.[38] The approaches of Moxter have continuously improved and eventually drove the Institute of Certified Public Accountants to create the so called Principles for the implementation of business appraisals (IDS S1).[39]

Compared to the proposals of Adolf Moxter, much less principles are enshrined in the standard of the Institute of Certified Public Accountants. This also leads further to the conclusion that even with the introduction of the IDW standards no fundamental standardization has taken place. The principles of proper business appraisal should be applied regardless of the

---

[38] Moxter, A. (1983) Grundzüge ordnungsgemäßer Unternehmensbewertung

[39] Institut der Wirtschaftsprüfer (2008) IDW Standard: Grundsätze zur Durchführung von Unternehmensbewertungen

selected method. Due to the different weighting of principles, also a shift between the small, medium-sized and large enterprises may arise.

The principle of relevance of the appraisal purpose, also referred to as adequacy of task, can have a significant impact on the execution of the appraisal and therefore has to be detected already before the appraisal business.[40]

According to the principle of appraisal of the economic entity, it is necessary to evaluate the company as a whole. An appraisal of individual parts of the company would be possible, but the total sum of the individual values would not match the value in a holistic appraisal.

In turn, it is necessary that both the operating assets and the non-operating assets are valued. However, there needs to be a separate appraisal. This makes a distinction between these two categories of assets necessary.[41]

The need for the subdivision and separate appraisal results also from the fact that the incomes from non-operating assets are not

---

[40] Raupach, A. (ed.) (1984) Werte und Wertermittlung im Steuerrecht, p. 388

[41] Kuhner, C., Maltry, H. (2006) Unternehmensbewertung, p. 43

included in the value of the company. In addition, these are not necessary for the company, so they can be sold easily without incurring negative effects on the company.

Accordingly, it is necessary that in addition to operating assets also virtual net sale price is included in the calculation of the operating assets. However, it will only be considered if this value is higher than the calculated income value.[42]

One of the fundamental problems in the appraisal business results, among other things, from consideration of the risk. In the following, this issue will be analized more closely.

From these information economists can derive initially, that both the events and the purpose of the business appraisal also have influence on the company evaluation. Because in the context of the classic methods the risk is considered only limited, there is a clear need for further development.[43]

---

[42] Lüdenbach, N., Hoffmann, W.-D. (2010) IFRS Kommentar: Das Standardwerk, 8. Edition, p. 415

[43] Metz, V. (2007) The capitalization rate in business appraisal, p. 77

Also, the absence of unambiguous statutory prevailing or standards in corporate value determination point to a more fundamental problem. This means that the determination of the business value depends on the respective evaluator and the used method, so that a significant range of corporate value is generated.

4   ACT OF THE BUSINESS APPRAISAL

4.1   METHODS OF THE BUSINESS APPRAISAL

4.1.1   The income approach

Economists typically fall back on the income approach in situations of company disposal. The result of the income approach should provide the prospective investor a starting point for assessing his investment opportunity. Thus, the potential investor may use the calculated income value for comparison with other investment opportunities.[44]

However, when comparing, he must note that he has to consider various factors such as availability, maturity structure and an uncertainty factor. Thus, the comparison with other companies is much more difficult.[45] The income approach uses as basis the capital value formula of the dynamic capital budgeting. Thus,

---

[44] Krag, J., Kasperzak, R. (2000) Grundzüge der Unternehmensbewertung, p. 35

[45] Mandl, G., Rabel, K. (1997) Unternehmensbewertung, p. 32

any positive capital value is considered a rentable and worthwhile investment.[46]

However, in order to calculate the income value for a future period, the economist has to take a discounting from the company's expecting gains by using the capital value formula.[47]

4.1.1.1 Representation of the risk in the income approach

For discounting the income value, the economist uses the so-called capitalization rate. With that he considers the buyer's expected yield demand. In comparison with other methods of investment, the capitalization rate generally follows the interest rate of the most profitable possibility.

In general, the capitalization rate has an important position in the calculation of the income value. Eventually it allows the comparison of different investments, among others, risk-free investments such as investing in federal loans.

However, the economist must consider that federal loans generally have only a term of ten years, meanwhile companies

---

[46] Behringer, p. (2001) The gross rental method for appraisal of small enterprises p. 719

[47] Sieben, G. (1995) business appraisal, p. 720ff

can achieve yields for the not limited period. This in turn raises the problem that there is no fixed rate available for a business. Therefore, the company can determine only an approximate value.

In the convergence solution, initially a risk-free interest rate is chosen as the basis and increased by a risk premium. This includes in particular the risk premium adjustments for the term, taxes as well as an uncertainty factor.[48]

To take account of the risk in the income value method, there are two different methods.[49] For the application of the risk premium method, the economist has to carry out a two-stage method. First, he must determine the risk-free rate as the prime rate. In the second step, the determination of an adequate risk premium follows.[50]

---

[48] Behringer, p. (2001) Das Ertragswertverfahren zur Bewertung von kleinen Unternehmen, p. 723

[49] Siepe, G. (1986) Das allgemeine Unternehmerrisiko bei der Unternehmensbewertung, p. 705

[50] Eidel, U. (1999) Moderne Verfahren der Unternehmensbewertung und Performance-Messung, p. 34

In turn, the prime rate depends on a country-specific long-term investment. In Germany, economists usually resort to a long-term federal loan with a term of ten years.[51] For example, the interest rate of the federal loans issued in September 2013 2.06 percent.[52]

The biggest problem in determining the risk premium is that it is at the discretion of the person carrying out the appraisal.[53] However, it is possible to perform a plausibility check of the noted risk premium under the use of various series of payments.[54]

In application of the security equivalent method, the economist replaces the expected surplus with the certainty equivalent in the calculation. The security equivalent corresponds to a safe

---

[51] Günther, R. (1998) Unternehmensbewertung: Ermittlung des Ertragswerts nach Einkommensteuer bei Risiko und Wachstum, p. 382

[52] Handelsblatt (2013) Germany zahlt höhere Zinsen

[53] Lüdenbach, N. (2001) Unternehmensbewertung nach IDW S 1, p. 600

[54] Behringer, p. (2001) Das Ertragswertverfahren zur Bewertung von kleinen Unternehmen, p. 194

amount that the owner has to pay to the investor so that he forgoes possible uncertain profits of the company.[55]

In order to calculate the security equivalent, the economist uses the benefit theory of Bernoulli, which is the basis for the application of probability distribution.[56] Therefore, the economist can calculate the risk premium after transformation of the gross rental formula.[57]

Considering the tax in the gross rental method, it is first necessary to distinguish between the personal taxes of the entrepreneur and the taxes of the company. Since the economist cannot make any definite statements regarding the level of private taxes, they must not be considered as part of the appraisal, as initially no influence is assumed on the company's value.[58] On the other hand, since 1997 the Institute of Certified

---

[55] Behringer, p. (2001) Das Ertragswertverfahren zur Bewertung von kleinen Unternehmen, p. 73

[56] Siegel, T. (1992) Methoden der Unsicherheitsberücksichtigung in der Unternehmensbewertung, p. 23

[57] Behringer, p. (1999) Unternehmensbewertung der Mittel-und Kleinbetriebe, p. 74

[58] Mandl, G., Rabel, K. (1997) Unternehmensbewertung, p. 170

Public Accountants suggests that the economist should make a consideration of the personal taxes.[59]

In this context, the Institute of Certified Public Accountants proposes to change the applied interest rate. This clearly increases the complexity of the appraisal method. In this context, there are also no further statements as to whether the modification of the interest rate would lead to an improved validity of the appraisal.[60]

However, in order to determine the company's profit, the economist must consider taxes which the enterprise has to pay by itself, such as business tax and - depending on the company's legal form - the corporation tax.[61]

The economist can carry out the calculation of the income value in several steps. In the first step, he calculates based on the last balance sheet for the future three to five years. In this first

[59] Siepe, G. (1997) Die Berücksichtigung von Ertragsteuern bei der Unternehmensbewertung, p. 1

[60] Behringer, p. (2001) Das Ertragswertverfahren zur Bewertung von kleinen Unternehmen, p. 723

[61] Siepe, G. (2000) Der neue IDW Standard, p. 952

calculation, the economist calculates the growth based on the last balance sheet and makes it a discounting of annual surplus.[62]

In further calculation, the economist considers a constant growth and carries out the discounting. In order to make the complete calculation, the economist has to remember the previously applied capitalization rate. Thus, it is basically possible to consider a growth in the calculation of the income value.

4.1.1.2 Consideration of the Substance of the Business Assets and the Non-Necessary Operating Assets

When using the income value method for the calculation of the enterprise value, the economist carries out a calculation, based on the future surplus revenues, which can be generated through the activity of the company. Furthermore, the economist also considers possible, hidden profit distributions while using the income value method.[63]

---

[62] Wiehle, U., Diegelmann, M., Deter, H., Schömig, p. N., Rolf, M. (2004) Unternehmensbewertung: Methoden, Rechenbeispiele, Vor- und Nachteile, 2. Edition, p. 28 and p. 34ff

[63] Baden-Württemberg / service-bw (not stated) Wertermittlung

However, due to the systematics used in the income value method to calculate the business value, generally the existing company's substance is not taken into account. This means that the entrepreneur can accept the customer's statement in this context.

The non-necessary business assets are all assets that are not needed for the actual performance of the company. This means that the entrepreneur can take these items from the company, without that this would have an impact on the operation performed by the company activity.[64]

In the simplified income value method according to § 200 BewG, the economist calculates the company value at the basis of the capitalization of the annual net profit as well as plus the non-necessary business assets and other assets.

---

[64] IHK Lüneburg-Wolfsburg (not stated) Vereinfachtes Ertragswertverfahren

4.1.2 Discounted Cash Flow Method

In the discounted cash flow method, the economist also uses the cash value for determining of the limit price. In order to do so, he first takes a bearing on the market prices, so that he can determine the market value of the equity capital used in the company.[65]

From this, the economist can deduce that the investment decisions of the equity owner or of the debt capital owner lead their focus on an minimum interest rate and not on a possible alternative investment.

In the discounted cash flow method, the economist makes differences between the equity approach and the entity approach. The equity approach is similar to the income value method, so that economists apply it neither in practice nor in theory. This means that for the business appraisal only the entity method is important, so that in following I discuss only the entity method.[66]

---

[65] Schmundt, W. (2008) Die Prognose von Ertragssteuern im Discounted Cash Flow-Verfahren, p. 12

[66] Schröder, R. W., Wall, F. (2009) Controlling zwischen Shareholder Value und Stakeholder Value: Neue Anforderungen, Konzepte und Instrumente, p. 43

The economist divides the entity method further into the adjusted present value approach and the weighted average cost of capital approach. The Adjusted Present Value approach has very high demands on the respective evaluator, so the economist rarely uses it. He can deduce from this that this method is not eligible for the appraisal of small and medium-sized enterprises. Therefore, in the following the focus will be on the weighted average cost of capital approach.[67]

In the entity method, the total value of the company is determined based on the so-called free cash flow. The economist carries out the determination before interest and after tax discounting and after consideration of the net investments. For discounting, he uses the ordinary, weighted average cost of capital. He calculates this from the equity and debt capital provider's weighted yield demands. Then, he determines the value of equity capital by subtracting the market value and the outside capital from the total value of the company.

---

[67] Ernst, D., Schneider, S., Thielen, B. (2011) Unternehmensbewertungen erstellen und verstehen, 4. Edition, p. 36ff

The free cash flow shows the expected profit of the company. However, in comparison to the income value method, the company achieves financing neutrality. This means that the entrepreneur has considered all cash flows in the business environment. Therefore, he has taken into account both payments to the equity and the debt capital providers. Free cash flow represents the total of the payment surpluses to the investor.

To determine the cost of equity capital, the economist determines an interest rate, which results from a risk-free and a risky share. For the calculation of the risk-free part, economists usually use federal loans. The risky part is typically calculated on basis of the CAPM model. However, in the context of this thesis this won't be analyzed in more detail. Though, for the borrowing costs entrepreneurs use covenanted interest rates.[68]

In the discounted cash flow method, the economist must consider corporate taxes. These are partially included in the free cash flow and are influenced, by the interest rates on borrowing among other things, as economists subtract these from the tax

---

[68] Ernst, D., Schneider, S., Thielen, B. (2011) Unternehmensbewertungen erstellen und verstehen, 4. Edition, p. 51ff

base. In this context, I have to note that the income tax of the company is not considered as part of the discounted cash flow method.[69]

In summary, I can argue that the discounted cash flow method is comparable with the income value method, if the economist uses same basis, namely the cash value. However, significant differences arise in the calculation of free cash flow, as in the discounted cash flow method also the lender's payments are included.

4.1.3 Substance Value Method

A further method for business appraisal is the substance value method. In the substance value method the economist determines the current market value of the assets. Thus, the economist evaluates all material objects, which form the substance of the company. The substance value represents a

---

[69] Ernst, D., Schneider, S., Thielen, B. (2011) Unternehmensbewertungen erstellen und verstehen, 4. Edition, p. 279ff

value that the economist should apply in the actual time to create the company in the same state.[70]

In this context, it was therefore often critically discussed whether it makes sense to consider only the capital locked-up in the company, rather than to evaluate the company's income. Today this is still evident from the fact that economists use this method only for the appraisal lowest value limit or an auxiliary value for the income value method.[71]

There exist different scientific approaches to determine a company's substance value, so that it can be noticed in the substance value method that no standardization of business appraisal is present.

From a business view, the substance value is the company's value at a particular date. Often enough, economists use the balance sheet of the company as a basis. First, the substance value of the assets positions will be evaluated. In the following this sum will be reduced by the liabilities of the company.[72]

---

[70] Kreyer, F. (2009) Strategieorientierte Restwertbestimmung in der Unternehmensbewertung, p. 21

[71] Mannek, W. (2012) Handbuch Steuerliche Unternehmensbewertung, p. 115ff

[72] Deimel, K., Heupel, T., Wiltinger, K. (2013) Controlling, p. 318

The economist can apply the substance value method, if the company has a significant share of fixed assets, such as real estate and machinery. Thus, he can take the hidden reserves of the company into account in a sufficient degree. Accordingly, the calculated substance value may clearly exceed value detected on the balance sheet. The substance value is also particularly suitable if the company wants to take out new loans, as this value also represents the lending capacity of the assets.

With the substance value method the economist can also consider the company's intangible value. These are the company's value, also referred to as goodwill, patents created by the company itself, and the quality of management, brand values or the customer base. However, the determination of the value of the intangible components depends on the particular evaluator and therefore it is not or limited objective.[73]

As already mentioned, economists rarely use the substance value in practice. This follows in particular from the fact that the continuation of the company and the related income are of

---

[73] Deimel, K., Heupel, T., Wiltinger, K. (2013) Controlling, p. 323

greater importance. Even if the economist can use the asset value as an auxiliary value, he should not use it as a single size for decision-making.

4.1.4 Multiplier Method

The basic idea of the application of the multiplier method is to make a comparison with other existing companies on the market. The economist has to make this market observation and collect or derive comparable prices or rates.

In order to apply the multiplier method, the economist must define multipliers first. Multipliers are variables which reflect the ratio between the observed price / rate of the a company's equity capital - possibly plus the observed price of the company's outside capital - and a reference value, often a success measure.[74]

For listed companies it is relatively easy to obtain information about the market price and values such as equity and outside

---

[74] Küster Simic, Dr. A. (2003) Theorien und Praxis der Unternehmensbewertung: Teil G – Multiplikatorenverfahren, p. 2

capital. If the evaluator has the opportunity, he can also fall back on comparable transactions.[75]

By using the multiplier method, the economist can calculate the enterprise value as follows:[76]

$$Company\ Value\ of\ the\ appraisal\ Object =$$

$$\frac{Observed\ Price\ of\ a\ comparable\ Company}{Benchmark\ of\ the\ comparable\ Company}$$

$$* Benchmarke\ of\ the\ valuation\ object$$

4.1.4.1 Corrections in the Multipliers Method

In order to ensure the comparability with companies of different sizes, there is a need to make an adjustment. Further adjustment is necessary in volatility as well as country-specific and market-specific conditions. With this adjustment, the economist can achieve a normalized level. In this correction, the economist eliminates possible extraordinary profits for example.

---

[75] Küster Simic, Dr. A. (2003) Theorien und Praxis der Unternehmensbewertung: Teil G – Multiplikatorenverfahren, p. 3

[76] Küster Simic, Dr. A. (2003) Theorien und Praxis der Unternehmensbewertung: Teil G – Multiplikatorenverfahren, p. 5

Basically the economist must always make sure that the reference variables relate to each other in a consistent relation and these always refer to the same appraisal dimension. This company's value in practice is increased or decreased by regularly surcharges or reductions to ensure the comparability of the appraisal object with the respective comparison company. This increases or reductions often are based on subjective experience of the evaluator and explain themselves, for example, by different growth views, marketability or influence possibilities at the appraisal objects.[77]

4.1.4.2 Rejection of the Use of the Multipliers Method

The application of the multiplier method is often criticized legally. In particular, criticism is that every company has a unique structure; this is not sufficiently taken into account by applying the multiplier method. Furthermore, it depends on the individual evaluators from which companies it will be used for

---

[77] Weimar, D., Fox, Dr. A. (2010) Die Bewertung deutscher Fußballunternehmen mit Hilfe der Multiplikatorenmethode, p. 14

comparison, therefore the objectivity of the appraisal is limited.[78]

The Institute of Certified Public Accountants considers this method in IDW S1 as an allowed standard. However, the Institute of Certified Public Accountants points out at the same time that the multiplier method should only be used as a complementary appraisal method and thus it has only the function to check the plausibility of the result of other methods.[79]

4.1.5 Net Asset Value Determination

In order to determine the net asset value, it is initially assumed that the company will be dissolved. Therefore, the appraisal of the operating assets occurs at the basis of the values, which can be achieved at the time of determination of a sale. Liabilities are planned together with the respective fee amounts.[80]

---

[78] Nestler, Dr. A., Kraus, p. (2003) Die Bewertung von Unternehmen anhand der Multiplikatorenmethode

[79] Hundrieser, M., Mammen, Dr. A., Sassen, Dr. R. (2012) Übertragung von Betriebsvermögen, p. 153

[80] Peemöller, V. H. (ed.) (2005) Praxishandbuch der Unternehmensbewertung, 3. Edition, p. 83

Since it is assumed, that the assets of the company are sold separately, this is often spoken as a single sale. However, the problem occurs that particular for special models, such as production facilities, no clear appraisal is possible.[81]

Furthermore, assets such as brand names, customer bases and the personal resources are not recognized in the determination of net asset value. In addition, others cost for the liquidation must be considered. These are usually obligations according to the social plan and taxes that may arise in the liquidation process.[82]

The liquidation value can be determined as follows:[83]

Liquidation value of the assets

- Transfer fee of debt

- Expected liquidation costs

= Liquidation value

---

[81] Timmreck, C. (2003) Unternehmensbewertung bei Mergers & Acquisitions, p. 16

[82] Timmreck, C. (2003) Unternehmensbewertung bei Mergers & Acquisitions, p. 16

[83] Peemöller, V. H. (ed.) (2005) Praxishandbuch der Unternehmensbewertung, 3. Edition, p. 83

However, in determining the asset value, it is a determination of the amounts would have to be spent to rebuild the company at the current stage. The used assets are initially divided into an operational necessary and an operational non-necessary category.[84]

The appraisal of the operating assets is carried out with the current replacement value. Thus, state, age and remaining term of use of each asset must be considered.

However, the appraisal of non-necessary operating assets will be carried out with the possible replacement value.[85] From this results following determination to calculate the substance value results:[86]

Replacement value of the operating assets

+ liquidation value of non-necessary operating assets

- debt while continuation of the company

---

[84] Ballwieser, W. (1993) Unternehmensbewertung, p. 169ff

[85] Ballwieser, W. (1993) Unternehmensbewertung, p. 169ff

[86] Peemöller, V. H. (ed.) (2005) Praxishandbuch der Unternehmensbewertung, 3. editon, p. 80

= substance value

If a bad result situation exists in the company, the result of the liquidation value may as well exceed the value at a continuation of the company. Therefore, the liquidation value of the company is usually considered as a lower limit value for a sale. If the prospective seller is not prepared to pay a purchase price that is higher than the liquidation value, he can be recommended to destroy the company.[87] However, social aspects, such as a social obligation towards the employees of the company are excluded.

4.2 POSSIBLE PROBLEMS OF THESE METHODS

4.2.1 Consideration of the Employer's remuneration and separate business assets

Often there is the problem that the effort of the entrepreneur to practice this job is not considered in the expense of the company. This leads to the problem that the calculated income value is sometimes much too high.[88]

---

[87] Timmreck, C. (2003) Unternehmensbewertung bei Mergers & Acquisitions, p. 16

[88] Appelhoff, Dr. H.-W. (2010) Planung und Umsetzung der Unternehmensnachfolge, p. 43

Thus, a potential acquirer would pay a price, which is too high and at the same time be working for the company or even hire an employee with a comparable qualification. Therefore, it is necessary that the economist takes the imputed wage into account while calculating the income value.

In order to set a realistic, imputed remuneration, initially the economist must find a basis for comparison. Fort that usually the payment is used that would be paid to a external manager with a comparable qualification.[89]

After calculating this value, the economist can recognize in the correction of the yield value, so that sometimes a significantly reduced income value results, depending on the company. Thus, the seller receives a lower sales price, however, there is a need to take account of the imputed wages, and otherwise the economist would carry out a sale at an inflated price.

---

[89] Appelhoff, Dr. H.-W. (2010) Planung und Umsetzung der Unternehmensnachfolge, p. 43

Because the object of the special operating assets is an object, which is held as private property, it is first possible, not to include this asset into a business sale.[90]

Insofar as the special operating assets will not be sold, it cannot be recognized in the company as voluntary business property anymore. Thus, this asset must be taken from the company as a profit-raising object.[91]

In this context, for example, arise the problems that the property of the company is part of the special operating assets, the building however belongs to the company's assets. Several solutions would be possible:

• The new owner pays rent for the building to the seller

• The new owner buys the property in addition from the seller

• The new owner sells the property to the seller, and changes to a new location

---

[90] Mannek, W. (2012) Handbuch Steuerliche Unternehmensbewertung, p. 233

[91] Frotscher, Dr. G. (2010) Kommentar zum Einkommenssteuergesetz, EStG Anhang 3 zu § 15 EStG,   Rz. 266

4.2.2 Expenditure of Time Business Appraisal

Depending on the company, a business appraisal can take a lot of time. In particular, it also depends on the assets the company believes to have. For example, the appraisal of a special machine can take a large amount of time because for such assets, usually there is no market and thus the economist cannot resort to market prices.

In addition, the appraisal also depends on the number of the company's evaluated assets as at the appraisal the economist cannot go back to the balance sheet value. Instead, he should determine a realistic value for each asset, for example by a comparison with assets available on the market.

In particular, the procurement of external information to determine the company's value may be associated with a high expenditure of time. Although, for valuation the economist can often fall back on values of subject-specific databases, this is not possible for each asset.

4.2.3 Critic on the Discounted Cash Flow Method

In particular, in consideration of the ever-changing factors in the markets as well as the continuously growing competition pushes, the discounted cash flow approach comes to its limits. This problem arises in particular by the rigid planning approach with the "expected scenario" cash flows.[92]

Applying this method, it is assumed that the evaluation object at any stage of life of the investment has the same present value. In reality, however, it is necessary that the management performance reacts to the changes in the market, so that the optimum value of the object of valuation can be achieved.

The behavior of management leads to a continuously change of the evaluation object result. Thus, this value can be different to the value that was determined using the discounted cash flow method and it can sometimes be significantly undervalued.

The flexible reactions of the management to new information cannot be quantified by using the discounted cash flow method. Accordingly, extensions, delays and cancels cannot be taken into

---

[92] Trigeorgis, L. (1996) Real options, managerial flexibility and strategy in resource allocation, p. 1

account. However, this is possible with the real options approach.

5 REALOPTIONS IN BUSINESS APPRAISAL

5.1 DEFINITION: REALOPTION

In 1977, Myers founded the term „real option". In Myers' investment theory, a transfer of the option price to the economy's real sectors takes place. This method makes an evaluation of the operational and the strategic choices possible, also known as real options.

According to Myers, each investment is an option first. In particular, it should contribute to the growth, so economists refer to this option as a growth option. Due to this growth option, impacts on the company's value and its financial orientation arise.

The basis of Meyers' theory on real options makes up the financial option price theory on the capital market. According to Copeland and Antikarov, the meaning of real option is, that a right for an option's execution for a previously given price and within a stated time period is possible. However, the execution of this option is not mandatory.[93]

Accordingly, this means that a company has the opportunity to invest in projects or goods. However, these investments can also be canceled, postponed or extended.

Copeland and Antikarov explain this in an example. In this example, a person undertakes a journey from A to B. In this context, Copeland and Antikarov point out that this person would not rely on a rough description of the way. Instead, the person would create a detailed map with the different possible routes or use a navigation device and take a radio for traffic jams and weather reports.

All of the traveler's actions listed above the economist may understand as a real option. The basic investments are the map, the navigation device and the radio. The investment should make possible that the traveler arrives as quickly as possible and without obstacles to the specified target. Thus, an investment

---

[93] Allgeier, H. (2002) Realoptionen: Das Handbuch für Finanz-Praktiver, p. 21

results in an increased flexibility, which in addition, the traveler also uses to save time and fuel costs.[94]

The investment made in the flexibility the economist can interpret as real options. This results in a value creation under uncertainty.[95] The value creation corresponds to the traveler's expanded maneuver as well as the saving of time that may happen while considering the uncertainty (traffic) during the trip.

According to Rams a real option arises, when the following requirements are met: If on the one hand, the right exists - or more generally, the possibility to use an upside potential of the economic returns - and on the other side, the downside risk can be limited at the same time - so the economist generally speaks of real economic option rights or simply real options.[96]

---

[94] Copeland, T., Antikarov, V. (2001) Real Options: A Practitioner's Guide, p. 5

[95] Meyer, B.-H. (2006) Stochastische Unternehmensbewertung, der Wertbeitrag von Realoptionen, p. 162

[96] Rams, H. (2001) Die Bewertung von Kraftwerksinvestitionen als Realoption, p. 157

Schäfer suggests in connection with real options that they represent a flexibility potential for companies in investments. Thus, further impacts arise on the management's or the respective investor's future maneuvers.[97]

Thus, all the investments made for goods in the real market, the economist classifies as real options. In this case, the respective management takes the choice. These decisions can lead to either higher yields or losses. On the other hand, the economist must note that it is necessary for the management to adapt actively to the constantly changing conditions.

For the respective management the real options have the benefit of increased flexibility. This advantage is especially of fundamental significance when the end of a project is not safe. According to Peemöller et al, a company has real options when it creates its own investment opportunities from the combination of the potential of the know-how, management and market position.[98]

---

[97] Schäfer, H. (1999) Unternehmensinvestitionen, Grundzüge in Theorie und Management, p. 388

[98] Peemöller, V. H. et Al (2004) Praxishandbuch Unternehmensbewertung, 3. Edition, p. 804

How the real options affect the company's decisions for and against investment, the strategy of management and the evaluation, will be described in the following part of this Bachelor Thesis.

5.2 REALOPTIONS IN THE COMPANY APPRAISING

There are two different possibilities, considering the real options in the company appraising. The first opportunity is to treat the company in its entity as an option. This assumes that the available figures depict the company's growth sufficiently.[99]

Provided, the economist uses this method, a categorization of the assets as call and liabilities side as put option occurs on the balance sheet. The economist can use the options on the assets side to increase the flexibility. Correspondingly, the options serve the management as basis for the decision concerning the execution time of investments.

---

[99] Kuhner, C., Maltry, H. (2006) Unternehmensbewertung, p. 289

A study made by Copeland et Al shows that present value of an investment, in which the assets positions are categorized as options, are 30 to 40 % above the present value of investments without such an option.[100]

The options on the assets side of the balance sheet can have different types of real options. On the one hand, the option insists on postponement, on the other hand also on expansion or restriction. In addition, the option asserts cancelling of investment as well as a growth option.

Generally, convertible loans, equity and share options represent the options on the liabilities side of the balance sheet. For the management, these options make an increased flexibility possible in relation to the raising of capital possible.

If necessary, there is a way to generate additional capital through the issuance of convertible loans. The holders of these convertibles generally have the option, to exchange them into

---

[100] Copeland, T., Koller, T., Murrin, J. (2000) Valuation-Measuring and Managing, the Value of Companies, 3.Edition, p. 343

the company's shares in a predetermined ratio. Accordingly, the classification of this option also occurs as a call option.

Considering the American Put, in principle, it should also be possible for the company, to conclude lease agreements. This means, that the lessee has the right, to cancel the lease agreement earlier by paying a fee or transfer fee of the lease object after termination of contract. On the other hand, The economist can describe this option as the European Call.[101]

The second possibility is to determine only the basic company values of the liabilities side of the balance sheet with the discounted cash flow method. Accordingly, the discounted cash flow method desists from considering opportunities concerning the company's synergetic effects as well as future developments.

With the help of the real options approach, the economist determines the synergetic effects and future developments, so that the values of the current real options represent the present

---

[101] Copeland, T., Koller, T., Murrin, J. (2000) Valuation-Measuring and Managing, the Value of Companies, 3.Edition, p. 344

value of possible room for maneuver as well as the choice of the management.[102]

The economist adds the real options, listed on the assets side of the company's balance sheet to the company value on the liabilities side. Thus, the total shows the company's total value.[103]

While determining the real options values, the economist has also to consider whether they are individual or related real options. Accordingly, he must assess the isolated options individually and add them up afterwards.

If the options are related to a certain base object or to each other, the economist must set up the option value from the portfolio of real options.[104] In this context, he should note not to add the growth rates and risks to the values of real options.[105]

---

[102] Dück-Rath, M. (2005) Unternehmensbewertung mit Hilfe von DCF-Methoden und ausgewählten Realoptionsansätzen, p. 160

[103] Myers, p. C. (1977) Determinants of Corporate Borrowing, p. 150

[104] Dück-Rath, M. (2005) Unternehmensbewertung mit Hilfe von DCF-Methoden und ausgewählten Realoptionsansätzen, p. 240

[105] Meyer, B.-H. (2006) Stochastische Unternehmensbewertung, der Wertbeitrag von Realoptionen, p. 166

In principle, the economist should note that not all real options could help to increase the company's value. For example, a replacement investment has no effect on the company's value. The real options only have an effect on the company's value when the following five factors are present at the same time. These are the factor of uncertainty, the flexibility of action, the irreversibility of the investment amount paid out, the right time of exertion and a capital value without flexibility near zero.[106]

Hereinafter these factors which form the basis for the maneuver and thereby contribute to the company's increase value will be described in detail.

The uncertainty according to the criteria of real options is the not existing knowledge regarding the future returns from the investment made. Both internal and external factors have influence on the uncertainty. On the other hand, the economist can quantify this risk as standard deviation from the expected value.

The external risks arise from the changes in the markets. Thus, when considering the external risks, the economist must take in

---

[106] Copeland, T., Antikarov, V. (2001) Real Options: A Practitioner's Guide, p. 14

account both, product life cycles as well as purchase and sales prices. However, the internal risks arise within the company itself. For example, a change of leadership can greatly affect the motivation of employees and with this also the productivity.[107]

However, the flexibility of action describes the management's responsiveness for current changes in the business environment. Especially in investments, it is necessary for the management to react on new information. Accordingly, a sufficiently large room for maneuver must be there in order to reduce the expenditure of decision-making to a minimum, after the examination of the available resources or capacities.[108]

The irreversibility of investment expenditure relates in particular to the so-called sunk costs. These are expenses for planning or marketing that cannot be undone anymore.[109] Compared to this, the investment objects can be sold again, even if usually at a loss

---

[107] Copeland, T., Antikarov, V. (2001) Real Options: A Practitioner's Guide, p. 14

[108] Copeland, T., Antikarov, V. (2001) Real Options: A Practitioner's Guide, p. 14

[109] Meyer, B.-H. (2006) Stochastische Unternehmensbewertung, der Wertbeitrag von Realoptionen, p. 163

in value.[110] Therefore, it is necessary to analyze all possible scenarios in advance in order to reduce the costs to a minimum.

Often, the capital value method is the basis for investment decisions. According to this process, an investment is worthwhile if the present value (NPV) of the investment is greater than zero. The economist determines the Net Present Value by subtracting the acquisition cost from the present value of the investment. The economist determines the present value by discounting the expected future cash flows with the discount rate.[111]

After calculation of the Net Present Values, the management can make the decision for or against an investment. With mathematical calculation, the economist should classify the management's responsiveness as low, since he can calculate security in advance. Provided the net present value is close to zero, the investment can be classified as questionable, so a management decision is necessary.

---

[110] Seppelfricke, p. (2003) Handbuch Aktien- und Unternehmensbewertung, p. 103

[111] Myers, p. C., Brealey, R. A. (2000) Principles of corporate finance, 6. Edition, p. 99

However, it cannot be derived in principle, also with a positive net present value, that investment leads to success. Here, in particular, the moment is important, at which the investment is made.[112] Myers and Brealey assume that the investment results in a higher cash flow when it is carried out later.

However, if a positive Net Present Value results and only a now or never decision is possible, immediately the call option should be performed. The performance of the call option, however, only makes sense if the future cash flows or their present value can cover the cost of the investment.

If the net present value is negative or close to zero and there is a high uncertainty, the management should postpone the decision initially and at the same time observe the market. If it is foreseeable whether the demand increases, the economy withdraws, the competitiveness can be improved, or the cost can be optimized, the economist can assume the optimum time for the investment.

---

[112] Myers, p. C., Brealey, R. A. (2000) Principles of corporate finance, 7. Edition, p. 622

Accordingly, internal and external parameters have influence on the company's future cash flows. The external parameters represent the demand and associated revenues. Meanwhile, the internal actions represent the decisions of the management at the "right" time. In this context, the economist should note that it is a major challenge for the company to determine the "right time" for the investment.

6 RECOMENDS ON DESIGN FOR SMALL AND MEDIUM-SIZE ENTERPRISES

6.1 INFLUENCE WHILE CALCULATING THE BETA FACTOR

In the literature, economists have examined the CAPM many times. With the help of empirical support, they examined the explanatory content in many studies. While doing this, they looked closer at the beta factor and underlied different market indexes. Also, they choose diverse return intervals (quarterly, monthly, weekly, daily) and used them on different regression lengths (1 year, 2 years, etc.). It can be seen that both the selected intervals and the respective days of the week have an influence on the beta factor.

Since the beta factor has an influence on the calculation of the company's value, the intervals and the selected weekdays have an impact on the company's value. For the calculation of the beta factor, it is necessary to select a suitable index or market portfolio first.

In this case, the optimal solution would be a market portfolio that covers all risky investment opportunities existing in the world. However, this solution does not exist; therefore, usually stock indices are used as a basis. Accordingly, the possibility exists to use either a national or an international index.

However, the selection of national index may lead to incorrect calculation of the enterprise value. In addition, Stutz pointed out that especially in smaller countries the risk should be determined on the basis of international indices.[113]

Koller, Goedhard and Wessels support Stutz's claims. These explain furthermore that the economist should always use international indices in order to avoid distortions due to differences in sectorial evaluations.[114]

However, the economist cannot determine a clear statement about the profitability of an index in contrast to another index. This is especially because the determination of the efficiency of

---

[113] Stutz, R. M. (1995) The cost of capital in internationally integrated markets – The case of Nestlé, p. 20

[114] Koller, T., Goedhart, M., Wessels, D. (2010) Valuaation – Measuring and managing the value of companies, 5. Edition, p. 253

a stock market index represents an intractable problem due to the fact that it is not possible to observe the market portfolio.[115]

It may be assumed that the efficiency of an index increases with the growing number of assets inside. Furthermore, a variety of choices also exists regarding the composition, weighting, rectification and calculation.[116]

However on the other hand empirical studies show that the beta factor is only slightly affected at a sufficient number of shares in the respective index. For example, Michael Winkelmann's study, in which the four German stock indices were compared, shows a correlation between + 0.97 and + 0.99. When considering this low bandwidth, the economist can confirm only a marginal impact of the stock indices' selection.[117]

---

[115] Zimmermann, p. (1997) Schätzung und Prognose von Betawerten – Eine Untersuchung am deutschen Aktienmarkt, p. 92

[116] Bleymüller, J. (1966) Theorie und Technik der Aktienkursindizes, p. 60ff

[117] Winkelmann, M. (1918) Indexwahl und Performance-Messung, p. 475

Even if the current indices - in addition to shares - include other assets, the calculation shows hardly deviations from the "normal" stock market indices. Also, deviations between performance and price index are scarcely recognizable.[118]

The choice of return interval which the economist uses to calculate the beta factor is of fundamental importance. Among other things, this confirms Scholes and Williams study, which was made in 1977 for the American market. In particular, for shares, which had a high level of liquidity, economists recorded a significant difference of the beta factor for monthly, weekly or daily determination. Scholes and Williams described this effect as Intervalling effect.[119]

---

[118] Ulschmid, C. (1994) Empirische Validierung von Kapitalmarktmodellen – Untersuchung zum CAPM und zur APT für den deutschen Aktienmarkt, p. 188

[119] Dörschell, A., Franken, L., Schulte, J. (2010) Kapitalkosten für die Unternehmensbewertung – Branchenanalysen für Betafaktoren, Fremdkapitalkosten und Verschuldungsgrade, p. 54

This suggests a further problem, since there is no standardized definition of return intervals possible. A confirmation for this gives also the contemplation of one and multi-period CAPM as well as the Arbitrage Pricing Theory.[120]

Accordingly, a variety of authors points out to select the holding period of an average investor, and thus a longer holding period.[121] The advantage of choosing a long time period lies in the favorable statistical properties as well as the circumvention of measuring mistakes. On the other hand, the selection of a long interval reduces the number of available data points in the current sample, thereby may occur, inter alia, an inaccuracy.

This again means to pay attention to the sufficiency of data points for analysis. However, the economist also must note that in an extended observation period also the probability of appearance of structural interruptions increases.[122]

---

[120] Zimmermann, p. (1997) Schätzung und Prognose von Betawerten – Eine Untersuchung am deutschen Aktienmarkt, p. 99

[121] Unter anderem: Möller, H.-P. (1986) Bilanzkennzahlen und Ertragsrisiken des Kapitalmarktes – Eine empirische Untersuchung des Ertragsrisiko-Informationsgehaltes von Bilanzkennzahlen deutscher Aktiengesellschaften, p. 25

[122] Sharpe, W. F., Cooper, G. M. (1972) Risk-Return Classes of New York Stock Exchange Common Stocks, 1931-1967, p. 52

This also confirms a clear correlation between the return interval and length of the selected regression. This leads to the conclusion that the economist may not set these parameters independently of each other.

Another issue that has an effect on the beta factor is the selection of a specified weekday. For the German stock market, among others, Zimmermann confirmed this in a study in the period from 1974 to 1991.[123] In this context, it must be pointed out that both Zimmermann's study and other studies are related to stock markets, so economists cannot derive any general statement for other stock markets.

However, they can derive that by choosing the beta factor, the respective evaluator can have a significant impact on the calculation in the company appraising. Therefore, he must be very careful in choosing the beta factor and eventually compare a few beta factors with each other; this holds the tolerance as small as possible.

---

[123] Zimmermann, p. (1997) Schätzung und Prognose von Betawerten – Eine Untersuchung am deutschen Aktienmarkt, p. 112ff

6.2 DESIGN OPTIONS FOR THE DETERMINATION OF THE COSTS OF EQUITY

In general, the economist can classify the determination of the capital cost as problematic. Accordingly, he must consider also the influences of the capital costs. In addition, it makes sense to consider the financial assistance when determining the capital cost.

Also to the question cannot be answered in general, in which way it is meaningful to use finance economics as a support in determining the capital cost. This is due to the fact that in the finance economics a variety of different ways of thinking exist.[124]

In order to identify the characteristics and functions of capital costs within the individual financial approaches, it is necessary to distinguish the different conceptions of research from each other first. Here, the economist can make a subdivision in the traditional, neoclassical and in the neo-institutional approach.[125]

---

[124] Schmidt, Finanzierungstheorie, p. 3ff

[125] Kloster, Kapitalkosten, p. 48ff

6.2.1 The traditional approach

Among other things, Schmalenbach gave reasons for the traditional approach. The focus is on a descriptive-pragmatic approach. This means for the economist to describe the facts of the real processes as completely and accurately as possible. Hereafter from these data, he can derive recommendations for practical use.[126]

However, since the economist must consider a variety of external conditions and involved stakeholders, it comes to a very high complexity of this process. This leads to the problem that it is almost not possible to derive general statements.[127]

Instead, usually only specific problems can be analyzed. Therefore, the focus of the traditional approach is also finding a solution for problems of a specific company.[128]

---

[126] Bartscherer, M. (2004) Investor Relations in Versicherungsunternehmen (-konzernen), p. 31

[127] Ermschel, U., Möbius, C., Wengert, H. (2011) Investition und Finanzierung, 2. Edition, p. 103ff

[128] Tiemann, K. (1997) Investor Relations, p. 82

However, the determination of capital cost in the traditional approach is of fundamental importance. The focus is not only on the measures safeguarding liquidity and a high creditworthiness. Also in the traditional approach, the economist takes into account, on what terms the respective company can raise the capital.[129]

This concept should promise an economical financing for the respective company. It bases on the assumption that the costs for the raising of capital are very important, if a company decides for or against an investment.

While determining the capital cost, the economist always considers an imperfect capital market. Accordingly, he must include a variety of financial instruments. There is an increased complexity, but the economist attempts an accurate quantification of financing measures and its payouts.[130]

---

[129] Tiemann, K. (1997) Investor Relations, p. 83

[130] Ermschel, U., Möbius, C., Wengert, H. (2011) Investition und Finanzierung, 2. Edition, p. 69ff

Despite the complexity, the economist can decide realistic about the variety of different costs and consider the complex financing alternatives.

On the other hand, it is not possible to determine numerically the individual cost components, particularly the individual components, since these do not always lead to a payout. This results in particular from the fact that in practice often it is not clear whether internal financing or financing by means of equity lead to finance costs or in what extent the economist should plan them.[131]

Accordingly, the economist has to made a more accurate assessment of the equity cost in the traditional approach. In this context, I should note once again that it is only an company-specific determination of the equity costs.[132]

According to Tiemann, the economist must consider for the stock corporation's capital increase the following components as equity costs:

---

[131] Tiemann, K. (1997) Investor Relations, p. 84

[132] Tiemann, K. (1997) Investor Relations, p. 84

a) "preparation expenses
   - Costs for general meeting
   - Costs for notary

b) Issue costs
   - Underwriting commission
   - Company tax
   - Costs for print of the shares

c) Costs for admission to official listing
   - Commission for admission to official listing
   - Print costs of prospect and publish costs
   - Charges for official listing of a security

d) Recurrent cost
   - Coupon service commission
   - Service for renewal of coupon sheets
   - Market regulation costs"[133]

In this context, however, there is the problem that the economist only can clearly assign the cost if they arise in an extraordinary general meeting. However, if manager discuss this topic during

---

[133] Transslation of: Tiemann, K. (1997) Investor Relations, p. 84ff

the annual shareholders' meeting, they cannot determine uniquely the cost, but would have to define them as a share of total costs.[134]

However, the determination of the borrowing costs in the traditional approach is much simpler. This results particularly from the fact that the economist knows the cost level as well as the period of the capital commitment in advance. In particular, because of the knowledge of the period, in the company the economist can use the annuity, the internal cash flow or the net present value method in a meaningful way.

This means that the problems that arise when determining the capital cost for an equity financing, not occur in the financing of borrowed capital. However, this does not mean that the consideration of borrowed costs generally proceeds in the traditional approach without any problems. However, in the context of this Bachelor Thesis, there will be no more attention to these issues.[135]

---

[134] Tiemann, K. (1997) Investor Relations, p. 85

[135] Tiemann, K. (1997) Investor Relations, p. 89

6.2.2 The Neo-Classical Approach

In the context of the neo-classical approach, economists use especially economic or micro-economic principles as a basis. As a result, they always take into account the factor of uncertainty and the behavior of each participant in the market.[136]

Compared to the traditional approach, the focus is on the monetary sectors. Furthermore, an integral consideration of the analyzed company follows. However, in the neo-classical approach, there is the problem of a number of assumptions that do not correspond with the real processes.[137]

The capital costs in the neo-classical approach are of fundamental importance, the economist uses them particularly as a basis for decisions. This relates both, to the decisions that are in connection with the procurement of capital as well as the decisions regarding the use of capital.[138]

---

[136] Tiemann, K. (1997) Investor Relations, p. 90

[137] Tiemann, K. (1997) Investor Relations, p. 91

[138] Burger, A., Buchhart, A. (2002) Risiko-Controlling, p. 2ff

In the neo-classical approach, the economist can consider the costs of equity in different ways. On the one hand, he can treat them alternative costs. On the other hand, there is a possibility to determine the costs of equity through a so-called dividend or profit model. Another possibility for determination of the costs of equity is the use of the Capital Asset Pricing Model.[139]

Accordingly, it is possible to determine different costs of equity, depending on the application of the models. However, this means also that - depending on the used calculation model - the costs of equity, which are included in each company's value calculation, can vary significantly.

When considering the costs of equity as an alternative cost is assumed that the investor has different options. These are usually an investment in the respective company and on the other hand, other forms of investment, such as for example a financial investment in a bank.[140]

---

[139] Tiemann, K. (1997) Investor Relations, p. 94ff

[140] Faust, M. (2002) Bestimmung der Eigenkapitalkosten im Rahmen der wertorientierten Unternehmenssteuerung von Kreditinstituten, p. 117ff

At first, as a basis the economist underlies a minimum interest rate, which usually corresponds to a risk-free alternative rate of interest. Accordingly, due to the increased risk, the investment in the respective company only makes sense if the asset offers a higher interest rate.

Another possibility for specification of the costs of equity is the so-called dividend model. The basis of this model forms the consideration, that the company's value can be determined by capitalizing of the future dividend payments by the respective investor. Here, the economist makes a discounting with a factor representing the profitability and risk expectation. This leads to the following formula:[141]

---

[141] Tiemann, K. (1997) Investor Relations, p. 96

$$AK_{t0} = \sum_{t=1}^{\infty} \frac{Div_t}{(1+r)^t}$$

with AK_{t0} =   current stock price

        Div_t =   dividend payments of the appropriate periods t

        r   =   discounting factor (alternative contract rate)

If the assumption is that a constant dividend will be paid in a growing company, the evaluation formula, known as the Gordon model, arises for a growing company:[142]

$$AK_{to} = \frac{Div_{t1}}{r - g_{Div}}$$

with Div_{t1} =   dividend payments of the appropriate period t1

---

[142] Tiemann, K. (1997) Investor Relations, p. 97

With the alternative contract rate (r), not only the demand of investors for a certain rate of return will be quoted, but also the costs of equity of each company. As a result, the economy insinuates that the investors carry out a comparison of the prices for different stocks for the price of AK_{t0}. Therefore the economist can determine the company's costs of equity as follows:[143]

$$K_{EK} = r = \frac{Div_{t1}}{AK_{t0}} + g_{Div}$$

with K_{EK} =   costs of equity rate

The costs of equity, will be treated in the context of the profit model in a way similar to the dividend model. Therefore, there will be no further focus on this model in the context of this Bachelor Thesis.

The determination of the costs of equity is also possible with the Capital Asset Pricing Model. The capital asset pricing model has already been discussed previously in this thesis, so that the

---

[143] Tiemann, K. (1997) Investor Relations, p. 97

determination of the costs of equity with the help of the capital asset pricing model is also considered in detail.

Independently of the application of the traditional or the neoclassical approach, the conclusion arises that the different methods may affect the costs of equity significantly. Accordingly, the changing costs of equity have an effect on the calculated company value, so that with the application of different methods, the economist can control its level.

6.3 DESIGN OPTIONS FOR THE DETERMINATION OF THE RISK FREE INTEREST RATE

The risk-free interest rate has the function of depicting the profits, achievable at the evaluation period of a capital investment, which is safe and term-equivalent to the evaluated company. To act as an appropriate comparative rule, the capital market investment, which forms the basis of a secure prime lending rate, must be free of default, inflation and currency risk.

Also, it has to be feasible at the evaluation period and have the same temporal structure of payments as the evaluation object and take into account the yield on the capital market adequately.[144]

Furthermore, the interest rate is important to determine the risk premium as a difference consisting of market yield and secure interest rate. In literature, practice and dispensation of justice for business appraisal, the view is consistently supported that the yields on government loans are most suitable for the determination of the safe interest rate, if they are free of default risk.

The alternative investment government loan is considered to be risk-free if it can be assumed that the State meets its interest rate and repayment on schedule and in whole.[145]

In addition, in order to eliminate the risk of inflation, the alternative investment and the payments which should be evaluated, must match in respect of internal purchasing power. The economist should assume either real or nominal sizes in the

---

[144] Ihlau, S., Duscha, H., Gödecke, p. (2013) Besonderheiten bei der Bewertung von KMU, p. 80

[145] Schmeisser, W. (2010) Corporate Finance und Risk Management, p. 20

payments which should be evaluated, and the internal rate of discount.[146]

Finally, the economist has to make sure that the payments of the alternative investment match the currency in which he must carry out the assessment. Otherwise, there would be a currency risk. To avoid interest rate risk it is assumed that the alternative investment is held until final maturity.

The principle of term equivalence resumes here. It requires that the cash flows of assessment and comparison objects extend the same period.[147]

A company that has to be evaluated, offers theoretically a cash flow for an unlimited period of time, therefore a comparable alternative has also to meet this requirements. If the expected payments from the company arise limited, the required term equivalency can be ensured by the choice of a capital market investment with corresponding final maturity.[148]

---

[146] Schacht, U., Fackler, M. (ed.) (2009) Praxishandbuch Unternehmensbewertung, 2. Edition, p. 213ff

[147] Schacht, U., Fackler, M. (ed.) (2009) Praxishandbuch Unternehmensbewertung, 2. Edition, p. 188ff

[148] Breuer, W., Gürtler, M., Schuhmacher, F. (2010) Portfoliomanagement I, 3. Edition, p. 86

For the choice of shorter (or longer) working operating systems, there is no theory-based evidence, as the economist has to consider explicitly the comparative share's reinvestment decision which has to be included (or sell decision before the due date). In this case, the comparative alternative would be subject to an interest rate risk.

In connection with the cut-off date principle it is discussed whether to use the current yield in a secure capital market investment for determination of the risk-free interest rate or a prognosticating, expecting return in future periods..[149]

Decisive in using a fixed date interest rate is that the amount is sought, which would have to be invested at the valuation date in an alternative investment in order to receive a cash flow, similar to one of the companies, which have to be evaluated.

So, therefore it is decisive, what amount a stockholder would have to invest in an alternative investment at the valuation date to achieve equally high amounts, such as from the evaluation object in a specific development time. Thus, the principle of time

---

[149] Matschke, M. J. (1979) Funktionale Unternehmensbewertung, p. 216ff

equivalence provides the reason for using a fixed date interest rate.

In principle, the economist can create the term equivalence by replication of the future cash flow, which has to be evaluated, with a bunch of zero bonds of appropriate maturity. These represent the investment of funds over a certain period without interim interest payments; they only lead to an appropriate (out) payment at the end of the term. However, the requirement of the term equivalence creates a forecast problem, which cannot be abrogated, if the period for the evaluation of the payment surpluses is longer than the remaining term of the alternative investment.

This may be the case for both finite and infinite periods. In the context of business appraisal, the economist must evaluate cash flows regularly for an infinite period (going concern principle).[150]

However, no bonds with infinite maturity are available as comparison object in reality. Consequently, the term equivalence cannot be guaranteed for a number of cash flows.

---

[150] Hassler, p. T. (2011) Aktien richtig bewerten, p. 114ff

This raises the problem of connecting interest payment: After the expiry of the period of the longest capital market investment, the reinvest of the free funds would have be assumed at the prevailing interest rates (revolving investment strategy). For this purpose, an interest rate forecast is essential.[151]

Jonas, Wieland Blöse and Schiffarth have another point of view; they speak with recourse to the duration of cash flows about a "misunderstanding". In their opinion, an independent forecast of a connecting interest payment is not required. As an explanation they refer to the concept of duration. In certain conditions, finite, but very long-running cash flows show duration that it is still within the range of maturities of the traded bonds covered by the spectrum. Besides the fact that the established conditions, in which the duration actually fulfills this condition, are very restrictive, already the recourse to the duration is not convincing. This is even then, if it comes in the required production of the

---

[151] Widmann, B., Schieszl, S., Jeromin, A. (2003) Der Kapitalisierungszinssatz in der praktischen Unternehmensbewertung, p. 801

term equivalence to the actual, rather than the evaluated average term of a cash flow.[152]

It should be noted that this violation against the date interest rate solely arises from the need for a pragmatic approach, since no bonds are traded with infinite duration. This means that the capital markets are incomplete in this respect.

To deal with this capital market imperfection, the determination of the interest rate can be divided in two phases. The first phase represents the limited period, which is still overstrained by the remaining maturity of the longest dated bonds. This is followed by an infinite second phase, which requires the prognosis of a terminal interest after the first phase. To determine the interest rate for the first phase, it is necessary to make sure, in which form interest rates, which should be observed on the market on the valuation date, should be described. For the second phase, the economist needs to determine first at which period it should start (phase definition). On the other hand, he should decide, whether to continue the fixed date interest rate of the bond with

---

[152] Jonas, M., Wieland-Blöse, H., Schiffarth, p. (2005) Basiszinssatz in der Unternehmensbewertung, p. 650

the longest term (implicit forecast) or whether, instead, to predict explicitly the connecting interest payment.[153]

Indirect Method

For practical purposes of the business appraisal it is necessary for the economist to find a rate structure that is able to specify an appropriate zero bond rate for each maturity period. A prerequisite for this would be the listing of a default-risk-free zero-coupon bond for each time to maturity.

Indeed, for the German capital market for example, there are only a limited number of such bond, and thus also only a few of the appropriate data points of a yield curve which should be determined. This complicates its use for purposes of business appraisal.[154]

In comparison to other countries the zero-coupon bonds are predominate on the German market. These allow only the determination of the profit structure curve directly. In order to

---

[153] Ballwieser, W. (2002) Der Kalkulationszinsfuß in der Unternehmensbewertung: Komponenten und Ermittlungsprobleme, p. 737

[154] Richter, F., Schüler, A., Schwetzler, B. (ed.) (2003) Kapitalgeberansprüche, Marktwertorientierung und Unternehmenswert, p. 24

derive a yield curve from this, the economist should use stripped bonds or a recursive formal method.[155]

The stripping of respective 10- and 30-year old German federal loans, this means, the separation of capital and interest claims and their separate trade, is possible since mid-1997. Here the economist divides a coupon loan in a capital strip and separate interest strips, so that the separate strips represent economical zero-coupon bonds with different maturity periods.

With this the possibility arises to determine immediately a real zero coupon interest rate structure based on the separated trading of capital and interest claims of German federal loans zero bond rates.[156]

However, its explanatory power is estimated as very low. This has to do with the relatively low liquidity compared to the one of the original coupon loans, which may result in risk premiums. In addition, the demand for strips distributes not evenly in all maturity periods.

---

[155] Hagele, J. (2003) Mit Sicherheit mehr Zinsen, p. 211

[156] Lindmayer, K. H. (2012) Geldanlage und Steuer 2012, p. 119

Regardless of the bond stripping, in the recursive method it is possible to derive zero bond rates from the empirically observable yield structure. Precondition for the recursive method is a perfect capital market, which has at least as many coupon loans as required maturity periods.[157]

If the economist transcribes the redemption and interest payments as well as the appropriate prices of the individual bonds in a linear system of equations in matrix form, he can determine the zero bond discounting factors either by recursive substitution (recursion) or by matrix inversion and multiplication with the price vector.

Since the discounting factors in this approach are not derived directly from zero coupon loans, but indirectly from coupon loans, they are also called derivative (synthetic) zero bond rates.[158]

---

[157] Rudolf, M. (2000) Zinsstrukturmodelle, p. 180ff

[158] Heese, V. (2011) Aktienbewertung mit Kennzahlen, p. 122

6.4 DESIGN OPTIONS FOR THE MARKET RISK PREMIUM

In particular, considering the current very low interest rates on the capital markets, which base on the current low interest rates, the calculation of the market risk premium is to be regarded as problematic.

The market risk premium is based on long-term empirical studies and thus on data from the past. Here, a comparison is made between the risk-free form of investment and long-term securities. For each difference, the market risk premium is derived.[159]

However, particularly since the recent financial crisis, there is a special situation. Accordingly, risk-free investments are preferred in the markets. This leads to the fact that the market risk premium increases. Thus, in order to evaluate a company, the economist has to select a market risk premium based on the upper values of the past market risk premiums.[160]

---

[159] Metz, V. (2007) Der Kapitalisierungszinssatz bei der Unternehmensbewertung, p. 203ff

[160] KPMG (2012) Kapitalkostenstudie 2012/2013, p. 30

The determination of the capitalization rate from a risk-free yield expected in future and a past-based market risk premium is the best estimate of a risk equivalent, future-oriented discount rate in a stable macroeconomic situation. Indicators, such as negative yields on inflation-protected indexed German government bonds or a yield of German government bonds below maturity period of congruent EURIBOR interest, point out that this stability (temporary) does not predominate. The usual practice of the assessment of the capitalization discount rate has to be questioned in the light of a new capital market situation.[161]

The best estimator of risk-free returns remains unrevised the observable yield of the German government bonds, as neither a low-risk form of investment can be identified, nor a market failure in the trading of German government bonds is recognizable. The increased demand for relatively lower-risk German bonds leads to the current low yields and is an expression of heightened uncertainty. Consequently, it can be assumed that (cp) the assumption of risk is remunerated on the capital market with a higher price.

---

[161] Metz, V. (2007) Der Kapitalisierungszinssatz bei der Unternehmensbewertung, p. 203ff

Therefore, in the determination of a reasonable, objectified risk premium it is temporarily advised to check in the business appraising whether the current situation accommodates the approach of the market risk premium on top of the recommended range of historically measured risk premium.

When considering historical market risk premium of 5 %, the economist can also derive market risk premiums of up to 9 %. This market risk premium in a short-term perspective is mainly affected by a changed inflation rate.[162]

Considering the current risk-free interest rate for a 30-year-old German federal loan in the amount of 2.5920 %,[163] it results in a market risk premium of 6.4080 %. This differs from the historical values of about 1.4 % to the top in a longer-term view.

In this regard, the Institute of Certified Public Accountants (IDW) recommended ranges from 4.5 % to 5.5 % before personal income tax and 4 % to 5 % after personal income tax.[164]

---

[162] KPMG (2012) Kapitalkostenstudie 2012/2013, p. 30

[163] Date of the Stock Market Price: 30.01.2014

[164] IDW (2009) IDW-Fachnachrichten, p. 696ff

Thus, it is in the discretion of the evaluator to determine the market risk premium in the calculation of the respective company's value. Taking into account the IDW-recommended range listed above between 4.5 % and 5.5 % and the consideration of self-identified market risk premium of 6.4080 %, significant deviations can arise. For example, if an enterprise value of € 500,000 were assumed, the market risk premiums would have the following amounts:

500.000 € * 4,5 % =   22.500 €

500.000 € * 5,5 % =   27.500 €

500.000 € * 6,4080 % =   32.040 €

Even in this supposedly low company value, a difference between the interest rate of 4.5 % and the interest rate of 6.4080 % in the amount of 9,540 euros can be seen. For larger companies, this difference increases accordingly.

6.5 DESIGN OPTIONS FOR THE DETERMINATION OF THE „GOODWILL"

Goodwill or the derivative business or company value represents the difference between the calculated yield value and the company's substance value. Accordingly, the goodwill relates to the share of the purchase price, which is paid in addition to the material available assets for constituents such as regular clientele, employees, reputation, brand or market performance.[165]

The height of the respective goodwill depends in principle on the industry to which the company belongs. For example, the goodwill in service companies is comparatively higher than that in companies in the manufacturing sector.[166]

Goodwill can be divided into the substantive and the personal goodwill. The substantive goodwill is connected to a fixed object. Accordingly, the factual goodwill includes factors such

---

[165] Velte, p. (2008) Intangible Assets und Goodwill im Spannungsfeld zwischen Entscheidungsrelevanz und Verlässlichkeit, p. 403

[166] Schmidt, I. M. (2007) Ansätze für eine umfassende Rechnungslegung zur Zahlungsbemessung und Informationsvermittlung, p. 270

as location advantages.[167] The personal goodwill, however, is paid for personal factors, such as the high quality of top management, its image or contacts.[168]

In addition, the goodwill can be divided in derivative and original goodwill. The original goodwill is an internally generated goodwill and cannot be stated on the balance sheet accordingly. The derivative goodwill, however, may be considered in the balance sheet, as it was for example purchased as part of a business transfer.[169]

The derived goodwill may only be written off in consideration of the IFRS standards when it represents no more value to the buyer in the future.

Thus, in the context of business appraisal, the derivative goodwill, which may arise from both personal as well as pertinent factors, is of fundamental importance. For the evaluation of goodwill, the economist takes the future profits of

---

[167] Heintzenberg, Dr. R. (1957) Die Einzelunternehmung im Erbgang, p. 123

[168] Knobbe-Keuk, B. (1993) Bilanz- und Unternehmenssteuerrecht, 9. Edition, p. 243

[169] Schmidt, I. M. (2002) Bilanzierung des Goodwills im internationalen Vergleich, p. 27

the company into account. Accordingly, this means a lot of effort and for some evaluators it can be very problematic.

Thus, the respective evaluator must consider factors such as the customer base.[170] In particular, when considering the customer base, the respective evaluator must consider whether these include active customers or just exist in the customer file, and have not acquired any products or services of the company for a certain time.[171]

In particular, it is also necessary for the evaluator to consider the average revenue potential of the customer base while assessing the customer base. From this, forecasts for the future and thus also for the determination of goodwill, can be derived.[172]

This also means that the respective evaluator can form an amount of goodwill especially in companies with a low share of fixed assets. This results in particular from the fact that there are

---

[170] Tanski, J. S. (2006) Bilanzpolitik und Bilanzanalyse nach IFRS, p. 97ff

[171] Ihlau, S., Duscha, H., Gödecke, p. (2013) Besonderheiten bei der Bewertung von KMU, p. 71ff

[172] Velte, p. (2008) Intangible Assets und Goodwill im Spannungsfeld zwischen Entscheidungsrelevanz und Verlässlichkeit, p. 191

no uniform valuations for factors such as customer base or reputation.

However, the goodwill, which the buyer pays ultimately, is not only influenced by the evaluator's calculations. Instead, it results rather from the negotiations between buyer and seller.[173]

---

[173] Haaker, A. (2008) Potential der Goodwill-Bilanzierung nach IFRS für eine Konvergenz im wertorientierten Rechnungswesen, p. 123

7   CONCLUSION AND OUTLOOK

In different situations, the business appraisal may be of high importance for the respective company as well as for its management or owner. This includes both, the business transfer or sale. On the other hand, further reasons, as for example borrowed capital or capital raise, can lead to an evaluation.

The collected information suggests a fundamental problem in connection with the company's evaluation. This is, in particular, that no single standard exists for the company appraisal. This refers not only to the Federal Republic of Germany, but can be seen as a global problem.

Although the methods used for business appraisal were standardized as far as possible, this does not mean that more evaluators would determine the same company value. Instead, several evaluators would determine a different value for one and the same company.

A difference in the goodwill is of great disadvantage for owners, especially when it differs too much downwards. This follows in particular from the fact that the value was determined by the professional evaluator, who - from the perspective of buyers and sellers - is considered as a basis for negotiations in a business sale.

However, even if the company will not be sold, a significant disadvantage for the owner can result from too low goodwill. This disadvantage is particularly given when the calculated goodwill is used as the basis for a credit rating or a credit. This allows the owner to receive either no credit, get a lower loan or receive a higher interest rate offer.

Even in matters relating to the tax law, in particular in an inheritance or donation, the amount of goodwill is also of high importance. Thus, a divergent goodwill leads to a significantly higher tax liability.

Not only for the particular buyer, the amount of goodwill can have a significance. In particular, a too high goodwill would mean for the buyer that he would have paid a too high price for the company. Therefore he requires a longer period, until his incomes have covered the investment.

Even if a uniform application of the previously proposed methods of business appraisal would be applied, further variations in the calculated value of the company could result from this. These differences could arise for example from the equity's interest payment, since even a range of one percent in high business values would possibly lead to differences of several thousand or several ten thousands euros.

To counter this fundamental problem of the company appraisal, uniform standards must be created. This means ultimately to create a requirement that only one of the methods may be applied in business appraisal. Also fixed rates for the equity's interest payment must be defined without a range.

However, it is questionable whether these rules would completely eliminate the problem. In particular, small and medium-sized enterprises, which are dependent on the manager - who simultaneously is often the owner - in a very high share, a problem may arise due to the central pooling of information and expertise. This means that a business sale and simultaneous retirement of the CEO would have significant influence on the company's value.

However, these factors cannot be considered by standard models. Instead, these influences are different from company to company and therefore must be taken into account by the respective evaluator in a different way.

Thus, no recommendation for any of the previously introduced methods for company appraisal can be issued. Instead, the choice always depends on the circumstances of the company which should be evaluated. This means in particular that the status of available information in the respective company must be considered.

Also the recommendations for the interpretation of each method and the associated factors depend on the respective company or even on its evaluators. Regarding this, also no general recommendations can be derived. Accordingly, the respective evaluator must also take into account the local factors.

However, a starting point for future research might be created here. In doing so, several companies would have to be evaluated by the application of the different methods. This would have the effect of changes in different parameters, such as a change in the market risk premium or a change in determined beta coefficient.

From this a conclusion could be derived, in how far the identified business values differ. In addition, it could be derived which of these methods can be most and which can be least influenced by the modified parameter. A low range despite different parameters could indicate that this method is preferable for the company appraisal. Thus, it could either be recommended that this method is preferable to other methods or derive a recommendation for the introduction of mandatory standards for business appraisal.

LIST OF LITERATURE

Akademie des Handwerks an der Unterweser (not stated) Schnittstelle zwischen Büro und Werkstatt (http://www.akademie-bremerhaven.de/index.php?id=382) Access on 15.01.2014

Allgeier, H. (2002) Realoptionen: Das Handbuch für Finanz-Praktiver, Wiley

Andreae, C. von (2007) Familienunternehmen und Publikumsgesellschaft: Führungsstrukturen, Strategien und betriebliche Funktionen im Vergleich, Deutscher Universitäts-Verlag, Wiesbaden

Appelhoff, Dr. H.-W. (2010) Planung und Umsetzung der Unternehmensnachfolge (http://www.ihk-oldenburg.de/download/vortrag_dr_appelhoff_unternehmernac hfolge_2010.pdf) Access on 05.12.2013

Baden-Württemberg / service-bw (not stated) Wertermittlung (https://www.service-bw.de/zfinder-bw-web/lifesituations.do?llid=1083932&llmid=0&language=eng) Access on 04.12.2013

Ballwieser, W. (1993) Unternehmensbewertung, Schäffer-Poeschel, Stuttgart

Ballwieser, W. (2002) Der Kalkulationszinsfuß in der Unternehmensbewertung: Komponenten und Ermittlungsprobleme, veröffentlicht in: Die Wirtschaftsprüfung, p. 736 - 743

Bartscherer, M. (2004) Investor Relations in Versicherungsunternehmen (-konzernen), Verlag Versicherungswirtschaft, Karlsruhe

Behringer, p. (1999) Unternehmensbewertung der Mittel- und Kleinbetriebe, Erich Schmidt Verlag, Berlin

Behringer, p. (2001) Das Ertragswertverfahren zur Bewertung von kleinen Unternehmen, Veröffentlicht in DStR, p. 719- 724

Bleymüller, J. (1966) Theorie und Technik der Aktienkursindizes, Gabler Verlag, Wiesbaden

Breuer, W., Gürtler, M., Schuhmacher, F. (2010) Portfoliomanagement I, 3. Auflage, Gabler Verlag, Wiesbaden

Burger, A., Buchhart, A. (2002) Risiko-Controlling, Oldenbourg Wissenschaftsverlag, München

Burkhardt, C. (2008) Private Equity als Nachfolgeinstrument für Schweizer KMU, Haupt Verlag, Bern

Copeland, T., Antikarov, V. (2001) Real Options: A Practitioner's Guide, New York

Copeland, T., Koller, T., Murrin, J. (2000) Valuation-Measuring and Managing, the Value of Companies, 3.Auflage, New York

Damhmen, A. (2012) Investition, Franz Vahlen, München

Deimel, K., Heupel, T., Wiltinger, K. (2013) Controlling, Verlag Franz Vahlen, München

Dörschell, A., Franken, L., Schulte, J. (2010) Kapitalkosten für die Unternehmensbewertung – Branchenanalysen für Betafaktoren, Fremdkapitalkosten und Verschuldungsgrade, IDW-Verlag, Düsseldorf

Dück-Rath, M. (2005) Unternehmensbewertung mit Hilfe von DCF-Methoden und ausgewählten Realoptionsansätzen, europäische Hochschulschriften, Frankfurt am Main

Eidel, U. (1999) Moderne Verfahren der Unternehmensbewertung und Performance-Messung, NWB Verlag,

Ermschel, U., Möbius, C., Wengert, H. (2011) Investition und Finanzierung, 2. Auflage, Springer, Heidelberg

Ernst, D., Schneider, p., Thielen, B. (2011) Unternehmensbewertungen erstellen und verstehen, 4. Auflage, Verlag Franz Vahlen, München

Europäische Kommission (2006) Die neue KMU-Definition (http://ec.europa.eu/enterprise/policies/sme/files/sme_definitio n/sme_user_guide_de.pdf) Access on: 05.01.2014

Faust, M. (2002) Bestimmung der Eigenkapitalkosten im Rahmen der wertorientierten Unternehmenssteuerung von Kreditinstituten, Tectum Verlag, Marburg

Frotscher, Dr. G. (2010) Kommentar zum Einkommenssteuergesetz, Haufe-Lexware Verlag, Freiburg

Grohmann, O. (2007) Integration der Informationstechnologie im Rahmen des Post-Merger Managements mittelständischer Industrieunternehmen, kassel university press, Kassel

Günther, R. (1998) Unternehmensbewertung: Ermittlung des Ertragswerts nach Einkommensteuer bei Risiko und Wachstum, Veröffentlicht in Der Betrieb, p. 382- 387

Haaker, A. (2008) Potential der Goodwill-Bilanzierung nach IFRS für eine Konvergenz im wertorientierten Rechnungswesen, Deutscher Universitäts-Verlag, Wiesbaden

Hagele, J. (2003) Mit Sicherheit mehr Zinsen, Finanzbuch Verlag, München

Handelsblatt (2013) Deutschland zahlt höhere Zinsen (http://www.handelsblatt.com/finanzen/boerse-maerkte/anleihen/bundesanleihen-deutschland-zahlt-hoehere-zinsen/8772612.html) Access on: 04.12.2013

Handke, M. (2011) Die Hausbankbeziehung: Institutionalisierte Finanzierungslösungen für kleine und mittlere Unternehmen in räumlicher Perspektive, Lit Verlag, Berlin

Hassler, p. T. (2011) Aktien richtig bewerten, Springer, Berlin

Heese, V. (2011) Aktienbewertung mit Kennzahlen, Gabler Verlag, Wiesbaden

Heintzenberg, Dr. R. (1957) Die Einzelunternehmung im Erbgang, Duncker & Humblot, Berlin

Hölscher, R. (2010) Investition, Finanzierung und Steuern, Oldenbourg Wissenschaftsverlag, München

Hundrieser, M., Mammen, Dr. A., Sassen, Dr. R. (2012) Übertragung von Betriebsvermögen: Erbschaft- und schenkungssteuerrechtliche Auswirkungen, veröffentlicht in Steuer und Studium, p. 148-153

IDW (2009) IDW-Fachnachrichten

IHK Berlin (not stated) Mittelstand in Berlin – Definition Mittelstand   (http://www.ihk-berlin.de/standortpolitik/mittelstand/818844/Mittelstand_Definitionen.html;jsessionid=06DC52567CC9E6548B80C1FC03070D2F.repl1) Access on: 05.01.2014

IHK Lüneburg-Wolfsburg (not stated) Vereinfachtes Ertragswertverfahren   (http://www.ihk-lueneburg.de/unternehmensfoerderung_und_start/unternehmensnachfolge/Unternehmenswert_-_ein_schwieriges_Thema/1200644/Das_vereinfachte_Ertragswertverfahren_nach_199_ff_BewG.html) Access on 04.12.2013

Ihlau, p., Duscha, H., Gödecke, p. (2013) Besonderheiten bei der Bewertung von KMU, Springer Gabler, Wiesbaden

Institut der Wirtschaftsprüfer (2008) IDW Standard: Grundsätze zur Durchführung von Unternehmensbewertungen (http://www.uni-hamburg.de/fachbereiche-einrichtungen/fb03/iwp/rut/BRC_IDW_Standards_SS11.pdf) Access on: 10.01.2014

Institut für Mittelstandsforschung (not stated) KMU-Definition des IfM Bonn (http://www.ifm-bonn.org/mittelstandsdefinition/definition-kmu-des-ifm-bonn/) Access on: 05.01.2014

Jonas, M., Wieland-Blöse, H., Schiffarth, p. (2005) Basiszinssatz in der Unternehmensbewertung, veröffentlicht in: Finanz Betrieb, p. 647 - 653

Kalmar, N., Sommer, U., Weber, I. (Hrsg.) (2013) Der effiziente M&A Prozess: Die Acquisition Value Chain, Haufe-Lexware, Freiburg

Knobbe-Keuk, B. (1993) Bilanz- und Unternehmenssteuerrecht, 9. Auflage, Verlag Dr. Otto Schmidt, Köln

Koller, T., Goedhart, M., Wessels, D. (2010) Valuaation – Measuring and managing the value of companies, 5. Auflage, Wiley, Hoboken

KPMG (2012) Kapitalkostenstudie 2012/2013 (http://www.kpmg.com/DE/de/Documents/kapitalkostenstudie-2012-2013-KPMG.pdf) Access on: 02.02.2014

Krag, J., Kasperzak, R. (2000) Grundzüge der Unternehmensbewertung, Verlag Franz Vahlen, München

Kreyer, F. (2009) Strategieorientierte Restwertbestimmung in der Unternehmensbewertung, Gabler Verlag, Wiesbaden

Kruschwitz, L., Husmann, p. (2012) Finanzierung und Investition, 7. Auflage, Oldenbourg Wissenschaftsverlag, München

Kuhner, C., Maltry, H. (2006) Unternehmensbewertung, Springer Verlag, Berlin

Küster Simic, Dr. A. (2003) Theorien und Praxis der Unternehmensbewertung: Teil G – Multiplikatorenverfahren (http://www1.uni-hamburg.de/Kapitalmaerkte/download/UnternehmensbewertungSoSe2003FolieG.pdf) Access on: 05.12.2013

Lindmayer, K. H. (2012) Geldanlage und Steuer 2012, Gabler Verlag, Wiesbaden

Lüdenbach, N. (2001) Unternehmensbewertung nach IDW S 1, veröffentlicht in INF, p. 596- 633

Lüdenbach, N., Hoffmann, W.-D. (2010) IFRS Kommentar: Das Standardwerk, 8. Auflage, Haufe-Lexware, Freiburg

Mandl, G., Rabel, K. (1997) Unternehmensbewertung - Eine praxisorientierte Einführung, Wirtschaftsverlag Carl Ueberreuter, Wien

Mannek, W. (2012) Handbuch Steuerliche Unternehmensbewertung: Vereinfachtes Ertragswertverfahren Aktuelle Erbschaftssteuer-Richtlinien, Walhalla und Praetoria, Regensburg

Matschke, M. J. (1979) Funktionale Unternehmensbewertung, Band II: Der Arbitriumwert der Unternehmung, Wiesbaden

Matschke, M. J., Brösel, G. (2005) Unternehmensbewertung: Funktionen – Methoden – Grundsätze, Wiesbaden

Metz, V. (2007) Der Kapitalisierungszinssatz bei der Unternehmensbewertung, Deutscher Universitäts-Verlag, Wiesbaden

Meyer, B.-H. (2006) Stochastische Unternehmensbewertung, der Wertbeitrag von Realoptionen, Wiesbaden

Meyer, J.-A. (Hrsg.) (2010) Strategien von kleinen und mittleren Unternehmen, Josef Eul Verlag, Lohmar

Möller, H.-P. (1986) Bilanzkennzahlen und Ertragsrisiken des Kapitalmarktes – Eine empirische Untersuchung des Ertragsrisiko-Informationsgehaltes von Bilanzkennzahlen deutscher Aktiengesellschaften, Poeschel Verlag, Stuttgart

Moxter, A. (1983) Grundzüge ordnungsgemäßer Unternehmensbewertung, Gabler Verlag, Wiesbaden

Müller, A. (2008) Anlageberatung bei Retailbanken, Gabler Verlag, Wiesbaden

Myers, p. C. (1977) Determinants of Corporate Borrowing, veröffentlicht in: Journal of Financial Economics, p. 147-175

Myers, p. C., Brealey, R. A. (2000) Principles of corporate finance, 6. Auflage, Boston

Myers, p. C., Brealey, R. A. (2000) Principles of corporate finance, 7. Auflage, Boston

Nestler, Dr. A., Kraus, p. (2003) Die Bewertung von Unternehmen anhand der Multiplikatoren Methode, Veröffentlicht in Betriebswirtschaft im Blickpunkt, Ausgabe 9, Seite 248

Peemöller, V. H. et Al (2004) Praxishandbuch Unternehmensbewertung, 3. Auflage, NWB Verlag, Herne

Prätsch, U., Ludwig, E., Schikorra, U. (2012) Lehr- und Praxisbuch für Investition, Finanzierung und Finanzcontrolling, Springer, Berlin

Rams, H. (2001) Die Bewertung von Kraftwerksinvestitionen als Realoption, veröffentlicht in: Hommel, v. U., Scholich, M., Vollrath R. (Hrsg.) (2001) Realoptionen in der Unternehmenspraxis, p. 155-175, Berlin

Raupach, A. (Hrsg.) (1984) Werte und Wertermittlung im Steuerrecht, Otto Schmidt Verlag, Köln

Rauter, R. (2013) Interorganisationaler Wissenstransfer: Zusammenarbeit zwischen Forschungseinrichtungen und KMU, Springer Gabler, Wiesbaden

Richter, F., Schüler, A., Schwetzler, B. (Hrsg.) (2003) Kapitalgeberansprüche, Marktwertorientierung und Unternehmenswert, Festschrift für Prof. Dr. Dr. h. c. Jochen Drukarczyk zum 65. Geburtstag, München

Rudolf, M. (2000) Zinsstrukturmodelle, Physica Verlag, Heidelberg

Schacht, U., Fackler, M. (Hrsg.) (2009) Praxishandbuch Unternehmensbewertung: Grundlagen, Methoden, Fallbeispiele, 2. Auflage, Gabler Verlag, Wiesbaden

Schäfer, H. (1999) Unternehmensinvestitionen, Grundzüge in Theorie und Management, Heidenberg

Schmeisser, W. (2010) Corporate Finance und Risk Management, Oldenbourg Wissenschaftsverlag, München

Schmidt, I. M. (2002) Bilanzierung des Goodwills im internationalen Vergleich, Deutscher Universitäts-Verlag, Wiesbaden

Schmidt, I. M. (2007) Ansätze für eine umfassende Rechnungslegung zur Zahlungsbemessung und Informationsvermittlung, Deutscher Universitäts-Verlag, Wiesbaden

Schmundt, W. (2008) Die Prognose von Ertragssteuern im Discounted Cash Flow-Verfahren: Eine Analyse der Decision Usefulness der IAS 12 und SFAS 109, Gabler Verlag, Wiesbaden

Schröder, R. W., Wall, F. (2009) Controlling zwischen Shareholder Value und Stakeholder Value: Neue

Anforderungen, Konzepte und Instrumente, Oldenbourg Wissenschaftsverlag, München

Schwarz, Dr. M. (2012) KfW-Mittelstandspanel 2012 (https://www.kfw.de/Download-Center/Konzernthemen/Research/PDF-Dokumente-KfW-Mittelstandspanel/Mittelstandspanel-2012.pdf) Access on: 16.01.2014

Seppelfricke, p. (2003) Handbuch Aktien- und Unternehmensbewertung, Bewertungsverfahren, Unternehmensanalyse, Erfolgsprognose, Stuttgart

Sharpe, W. F., Cooper, G. M. (1972) Risk-Return Classes of New York Stock Exchange Common Stocks, 1931-1967, Financial Analysis Journal, No. 2 / 1972

Sieben, G. (1995) Unternehmensbewertung, in: Internationale Wirtschaftsprüfung, Festschrift für Hans Havermann, IDW Verlag, Düsseldorf

Siegel, T. (1992) Methoden der Unsicherheitsberücksichtigung in der Unternehmensbewertung, veröffentlicht in: WiSt, p. 21-26

Siepe, G. (1986) Das allgemeine Unternehmerrisiko bei der Unternehmensbewertung, veröffentlicht in Der Betrieb, p. 705-708

Siepe, G. (1997) Die Berücksichtigung von Ertragsteuern bei der Unternehmensbewertung, veröffentlicht in WPg, p. 1-10 und 37-44

Siepe, G. (2000) Der neue IDW Standard, veröffentlicht in WPg, p. 946-960

Spielmann, N. (2012) Internationale Corporate Governance: Best Practice Empfehlungen für Klein- und Mittelunternehmen, Haupt Verlag, Bern

Stutz, R. M. (1995) The cost of capital in internationally integrated markets – The case of Nestlé, International Financial Management Nr. 1 / 1995

Sygusch, F. (2008) Nachfolgefinanzierung mittelständischer Unternehmen: Finanzierungsinstrumente und Gestaltungsmöglichkeiten, Salzwasser-Verlag, Paderborn

Tanski, J. S. (2006) Bilanzpolitik und Bilanzanalyse nach IFRS, Verlag Franz Vahlen, München

Timmreck, C. (2003) Unternehmensbewertung bei Mergers & Acquisitions, Hans-Böckler-Stiftung, Düsseldorf

Trigeorgis, L. (1996) Real options, managerial flexibility and strategy in resource allocation, MIT Press, London

Ulschmid, C. (1994) Empirische Validierung von Kapitalmarktmodellen – Untersuchung zum CAPM und zur APT für den deutschen Aktienmarkt, Lang Verlag, Frankfurt

Velte, p. (2008) Intangible Assets und Goodwill im Spannungsfeld zwischen Entscheidungsrelevanz und Verlässlichkeit, Deutscher Universitäts-Verlag, Wiesbaden

Wallau, F. (2006) Mittelständische Unternehmen in Deutschland, veröffentlicht in: Schauf, M. (Hrsg.) (2006) Unternehmensführung im Mittelstand, Hampp, München

Wassermann, B. (2012) 3. FOM Mittelstandsforum: Steuern, Recht & Bewertung (http://www.fom.de/fileadmin/fom/downloads/Tagungsbaende/ FOM_Mittelstandsforum_2012_Tagungsband_ONLINE.pdf) Access on: 15.01.2014

Weimar, D., Fox, Dr. A. (2010) Die Bewertung deutscher Fußballunternehmen mit Hilfe der Multiplikatoren Methode,

Schriften zur Finanzwirtschaft, Heft 7, Technische Universität Ilmenau

Welsh/White, A small business is not a little big business, in: Harvard Business Review, 59/80

Widmann, B., Schieszl, p., Jeromin, A. (2003) Der Kapitalisierungszinssatz in der praktischen Unternehmensbewertung, veröffentlicht in: Finanz Betrieb, p. 800 - 810

Wiehle, U., Diegelmann, M., Deter, H., Schömig, p. N., Rolf, M. (2004) Unternehmensbewertung: Methoden, Rechenbeispiele, Vor- und Nachteile, 2. Auflage, cometis publishing, Wiesbaden

Winkelmann, M. (1918) Indexwahl und Performance-Messung, veröffentlicht in: Göppl, H., Henn, R. (Hrsg.) Geld, Banken und Versicherungen, Verlag Versicherungswirtschaft, Athenäum

Wöltje, J. (2012) Finanzkennzahlen der Unternehmensbewertung, Haufe-Lexware, Freiburg

Zimmermann, p. (1997) Schätzung und Prognose von Betawerten – Eine Untersuchung am deutschen Aktienmarkt, Uhlenbruch Verlag, Bad Soden im Taunus

www.ingramcontent.com/pod-product-compliance
Lightning Source LLC
Chambersburg PA
CBHW060040210326
41520CB00009B/1208